Faith for the Future

Also by Colin Urquhart

In Christ Jesus
Anything You Ask
My Father Is the Gardener
When the Spirit Comes

COLIN URQUHART

Faith for the Future

HODDER AND STOUGHTON
LONDON SYDNEY AUCKLAND TORONTO

British Library Cataloguing in Publication Data

Urquhart, Colin
Faith for the future.
1. Christian life   2. Faith
1. Title
248.4   BV4501.2

ISBN 0 340 32262 4

*To Caroline, my dear wife,
who has loved and supported me
as together the Lord has taught
us to have faith for the future.*

Acknowledgements

The life of faith can only be learned in fellowship with others. I want to express my deep gratitude in the Lord to all in the Bethany Fellowship with whom I am learning to live by the principles of faith. Especially I want to mention David Brown with whom I have shared so much in prayer and fellowship.

My thanks also to those who have worked so hard on the typescript, particularly Esther, Elaine, Paul, Marigold, Vivienne and Cathy.

I praise God for Caroline, my children, Claire, Clive and Andrea and the household with whom I share my life, Vivienne, Annette, Anne and Jeremy. Thank you for all your love and encouragement.

The Scripture references are taken from the New International Version, except where stated.

Contents

CONTENTS

1   This Is to Encourage You

THE DEED OF Resignation lay in the drawer of my desk for several days; I could not bring myself to sign it. I would have to eventually, of that I was sure; but the implications of putting my signature to that document seemed immense. Never had God asked of me a greater act of faith.

I would be signing away my security, my job, the house where my family and I lived and the income that I received. However, these were not the main considerations that occupied my thoughts. It was far more difficult to see how I could leave the loving fellowship of people that God had created during the previous five and a half years.

I had become vicar of St. Hugh, Lewsey, Luton in 1970. Since then the life of that congregation had been transformed; people had been filled with the Holy Spirit, and many had experienced a considerable amount of healing in their lives. We had been faced with the commitment involved in loving one another as Jesus loves us. Together we had begun to count the cost of what it meant to lay down our lives for our friends. Instead of being churchgoers we were becoming a meaningful expression of the Body of Christ.

For over five years my family had become deeply integrated with the family of Jesus in that parish. Never had we experienced such fellowship, nor known that it was possible to enjoy such deep relationships in the Lord. Now it seemed that we had to leave those we had come to love so dearly.

Signing that Deed of Resignation was irrevocable; it contained a clause to that effect.

Some had advised against me leaving this parish. After all, it was said, God had accomplished a sovereign work there, which had been a great encouragement to many other churches. It was certainly true that we were constantly beseiged by visitors who came seeking a personal relationship with the Lord, wanting to be baptised in the Holy Spirit, or to receive healing. At times it was like living in a goldfish bowl with many people watching our every move.

The steady flow of miracles and healings had attracted considerable attention, and news of what was happening at St. Hugh's had spread far and wide. I was receiving many invitations to speak on parish renewal in the power of the Holy Spirit.

"You can't leave," I was told by some men of God whom I respected deeply; "the church will not be the same without you." I parried this suggestion by saying that the work did not depend on me; it was the work of God's Holy Spirit. I might be leaving the parish but the Holy Spirit would not!

There were even more who said that it was right for me to leave; they could see that God was calling me to a wider ministry. Events were making that obvious and the Lord was giving them witness that this was His purpose for me.

I would have to sign the Deed of Resignation. Deep down in my heart I knew it. Not that this was a hasty decision: it was one made before the world was created and had been revealed to me by the Lord several years previously.

Before beginning my ministry at St. Hugh's, I had experienced a release of the love and power of the Holy Spirit that was to transform my life. There was a great increase of love in my heart for both God and people, and also a new note of authority that had not been present in my ministry previously. Things now happened to people when I was ministering to them, in a way that I had not known before. It was almost bewildering.

People were meeting with Jesus personally. Their lives were being filled with the love of the Holy Spirit. I was praying with people for healing and seeing miracles happen before my eyes.

THIS IS TO ENCOURAGE YOU11

By God's anointing the Scriptures were coming to life for me and others in a new way; and God was enabling me to teach from His Word as never before.

Many prayer and healing groups were started in the parish and we saw God answer prayer in wonderful ways. Events were taking place at such a rate that it was difficult to keep pace with everything.

It seemed that I had been placed in an entirely different spiritual world from the one I had known previously. I was now experiencing things daily that I did not know were possible. And one of the most important of these was the ability to hear God speak clearly.

People often ask how you can know when the Lord speaks to you. Do you hear an audible voice? How do you know that you are not listening to yourself or to the enemy? How can you be sure that it is God?

It is impossible to give a satisfactory answer to such questions briefly: perhaps this whole book will offer at least a partial answer. The great men of God have often spoken about "the witness of the Spirit". Since this meeting with God I have had a quiet, but very positive, witness when God is speaking to me. Somehow I know it is the Lord. He may be speaking through the Bible, in a time of prayer, in a sermon, or simply through someone in conversation. At the same time, I experience a grave disquiet if what I am hearing is not from God. I am not at peace if my thoughts, even, are not right. If I say something that is wrong I experience immediate correction from the Holy Spirit and have to amend what was said.

This sounds very subjective, for hearing God personally must be a subjective experience. However, I am not talking of feelings, which can be very misleading as our emotions change so readily in response to what is happening around us. Hearing God is not a feeling; it is an inner knowing that the Lord has spoken. However, what is heard subjectively must be tested objectively. I have learned not to act impulsively but for many years have written down what I believe God has said to me. Then I test that by every possible means; I continue to listen. I know that what I have written is not the infallible Word of God; Paul says that our prophecy is imperfect. But I know that what is right will be confirmed by God through Scripture, through others and through the events to which His prophetic word refers.

Any Christian who earnestly wants to follow the Lord must be a listening person. For years before going to St. Hugh's I had learned to spend time daily waiting upon God, seeking to know His voice. Slowly in that time I had learned to distinguish what He was saying from other thoughts and words.

When the Holy Spirit was released in power in my life, one result was that I was able to hear God more clearly and readily. When I prayed, He was there waiting to speak to me. When I was going about my pastoral duties, He was there telling me what to say and do. More than that, He was speaking through me in a way that I had not known before.

None of this was an occasion for pride. For years I had been seeking such an intimate walk with the Lord, and now it seemed so wonderful and so delicate I wanted to do nothing that would cause His presence to recede or the clarity of His voice to be dimmed. Hearing the Lord in His Word and through prayer was so precious; I was awed at the privilege God had given me.

At first I was very unbelieving; I found it difficult to accept that God could speak so simply and readily to a nobody like me. But the things He was impressing upon me really happened. For example, when praying for healing, I would be aware sometimes that it was necessary to pray for something totally different from the need expressed. I would check what I was sensing with the person, and when we prayed in the way that the Spirit was indicating, the healing would take place.

People are understandably sceptical of anyone claiming a "hot line to heaven"; but God does speak to His children and He does expect them to hear Him. Yet I have found the whole business of hearing the Lord has been severely tested at times. It has not always been easy, often because of the seemingly impossible things He has said. People are rightly cautious of those who act independently upon personal revelation. It is important to obey the teaching of Scripture that everything be properly tested.

I had not been at St. Hugh's long when the Lord spoke to me one day more clearly than ever before. It was the nearest I had ever come to hearing an audible voice from heaven. "Your voice must be heard among the nations, and if you do not speak my people will not hear."

My immediate response was of utter disbelief and a desire to reject completely what had been said. It seemed preposterous. Here was I, a young minister with only six years' pastoral experience and newly in charge of a parish, with no other ambition than to be a faithful parish priest. I had no ambition to travel, no desire or calling to work overseas, and was totally unaware of any global move of the Holy Spirit.

And yet I could not dismiss these words. They had been spoken. They had not come from my own heart; they were far too outrageous. I comforted myself with the thought that if they were from the Lord He would cause them to come true. There was nothing I could do to make such a thing happen, and nothing could have been further from my desires. I was a very shy and retiring person. The thought of travelling and speaking to nations positively horrified me. And yet God had spoken and I knew it.

I did not even tell Caroline, my wife. She still did not know the Lord personally, was totally perplexed by all that was happening around her at St. Hugh's, and she was having to cope with being a vicar's wife and caring for three young children, all at the same time. And besides, I had assured her when we arrived that we would be at St. Hugh's for at least ten years; I did not believe in clergy hopping from one church to another!

Graciously, the Lord showed me that He had spoken in this way to impress upon me that my ultimate ministry would not be at St. Hugh's. I was to follow faithfully the leading of His Spirit while I was there; but there would come the time when He would lead me into the ministry for which He was preparing me.

In the pressure of events I buried all thoughts of the future and devoted myself totally to the job in hand. About twice a year, the Lord would speak again of the future — just to remind me of His purpose.

One such occasion was different from all others. It was All Saints' Day, November 1st, 1974. Again the Lord reminded me that my voice was to be heard among the nations. This was His calling upon my life and now the time had come to prepare me to move out into this wider ministry.

My immediate reaction was, "Not yet, Lord. It's too soon. I'm not ready, nor is the parish." But you can't argue with the Lord and win. Even in Scripture the call of God came to men long before they considered themselves prepared. This time I could not forget what God was saying, nor push it away. Every time I prayed I knew it was futile to resist Him.

At least I could now confide in Caroline. Within the last four years she had come to the Lord, been baptised in the Holy Spirit and was giving herself fully to others in the community life which we had been living for some time. Whatever the future held we would be able to face together.

I had thoroughly enjoyed the pastoral ministry; now I began to be very unsettled. Instead, I felt at home when speaking at large assemblies and conferences. It was then that I knew that I was fulfilling my true ministry.

Besides the three ordained members of staff at St. Hugh's there were six full-time lay-workers. They were responsible for administration and helped with pastoral visiting. Although the church had become a national centre of renewal, the congregation was a local one. The people lived in the locality and most had come to know the Lord at St. Hugh's. Many had been reached through our evangelistic teaching sessions, called "Know Jesus" groups, and through the lay visiting contact with non-believers. We were not interested in gathering all the "alive" people from the district. Many visited for our Sunday evening services, but we did not allow people to leave the churches to which they belonged. They were to be part of the Body of Christ in the place where they lived. If they needed to come to us for teaching and ministry so that they could be more effective in their witness, that was understandable; but they were not to come and join us.

What a strange reversal of roles. In the early years of my ministry I had been encouraging folk to join us; now I was telling hundreds of people not to!

The pastoral oversight of the parish was shared by the ordained clergy with about ten lay people, known as the leadership group, which met one evening every week listening to the Lord and bringing before Him any pastoral matter that caused concern.

During the week, most of the church family met in fellowship groups to share their lives in every way that was meaningful. They not only prayed together and studied the Word of God, but also ministered to one another and shared any practical or financial need. About fifty people were living in community and shared everything in common.

When someone was in need he would contact the leader of his fellowship group, who in turn would relay the information. Within a few minutes the whole group would be appraised of the situation and would be lifting the brother or sister to God in prayer.

If the matter was of greater moment the group leader would contact the parish office. From there all the other group leaders would be informed and would immediately notify the members of their groups.

If the matter was considered sufficiently grave, everyone would be called together to pray in the church building on that same evening. This was not often necessary, but I found such times deeply moving. When such an evening of prayer was called, all other activities would be cancelled and the building would be full of praying people.

The next time such a meeting was necessary it could be for me or a member of my family. How comforting it was to know that people felt so committed to one another that they would cancel everything else and come together to seek the Lord on the behalf of a brother; and many would have begun to fast as soon as they heard of the need.

Would I really have to leave such a fellowship of love? As I looked around the worshipping congregation on Sundays, my heart would overflow in thanksgiving to God. "Lord, you are so good! Look what you have done with us. Praise you!" I could see Jesus on faces, something of His peace, His joy, His radiance and His glory. I was aware of the great transformation that had happened in most lives and the miracles of healing that many had experienced. Was I really to leave them all?

The Lord's answer to me was clear: "I have other sheep, not of this fold. To them I am sending you." And when you are sent by God you have to go.

I made an appointment to see my bishop. Robert Runcie, now Archbishop of Canterbury, was then Bishop of St. Albans. I had enjoyed a good relationship with him throughout my time at St. Hugh's. He was quietly supportive of all that the Spirit was doing among us and encouraged others in the diocese to come and experience what was happening there. He trusted me to ensure that the ministry at St. Hugh's remained balanced and sensitive.

As I outlined what I believed to be God's purpose, he responded with sadness and yet agreement. "What God has given you must be shared with the whole Church," he said. Choosing a successor would not be easy, because few others had experienced the corporate commitment to which we had been led.

We discussed whether it was right for me to continue to be part of the Body at St. Hugh's while fulfilling my new ministry. We decided against this, a decision for which I was to be thankful.

I did not announce my departure to the congregation, as is usually done when a minister leaves. Such a thing would have been unthinkable. Within the Body of Christ our lives belonged to one another and God had taught us much, not only about our submission to His authority, but also what it meant to be submitted to one another. So at the parish's Annual Meeting, I explained what I believed to be the Lord's purpose, that I should leave St. Hugh's to fulfil a full-time itinerant ministry. Every member of the congregation was asked to pray and seek the Lord concerning this. Most were praying people who had been taught how to wait upon the Lord and listen to Him. If this was God's purpose, the Spirit would witness that to His people. My only desire was to do what He wanted.

There is always the danger of hearing only what you want to hear. God had brought us a long way together in the past five years and there would be much fear of the consequences if I was to depart. Yet I knew that God could overcome the fears within people and speak clearly to them of His purpose.

As they began to pray, people received immediately the witness that it was right for me to leave. One person after another came to me and said: "I don't want you to go, but I know that it is right that you do." Almost without exception the witness was the same. However, as they faced the implications for the future, some began to listen to their fears and asked me not to go. Only when they resigned themselves to the Lord's will did He deal with their fear and bring them peace. There was no escaping what he was saying.

That whole process took from April to September. Then I wrote to the bishop saying that the final decision had been made and that I felt it right to leave the parish at the end of the year. His reply was warm and he asked me to see him again prior to my departure. Meanwhile he would see that the necessary Deed of Resignation would be drawn up for my signature.

That Deed of Resignation! It had to be signed. Despite all the assurances God had given me, I must confess that it was with reluctance that I took the document from the drawer of my desk and added my signature. There, it was done! Now there could be no turning back. Goodbye security. Goodbye St. Hugh's and the people I had come to love so dearly.

For my family and myself the Lord would now be our security. Our future was in His hands. It was exciting, it was daunting, but it was right.

At least we had a house to live in. We were offered the use of one belonging to the Fountain Trust, by Tom Smail, their new director. This was situated at East Molesey, Surrey, and would be big enough for my family plus the two single people who would come with us to share our life and ministry.

Those who visited St. Hugh's experienced the holy presence of God in our midst and the obvious working of His Spirit. Whenever I was asked to minister in other places I was graciously received and welcomed. People seemed to rejoice in the fact that God was doing a mighty work in an Anglican parish. Now the Lord made it clear that my security was to be completely in Him, not in men; not in the Church as an institution, not in the system of which I was a part, but in Him personally. I would need faith for the future. He made it clear I was appointed to this new ministry by Him, not by men. This appointment would be recognised by others when it was seen that His hand was upon me.

I was determined that the last weeks at St. Hugh's would not be filled with farewell parties and events. The Lord needed to be at the centre of my departure as we had sought to keep Him at the centre of our corporate life. The four Sunday evening services prior to Christmas were devoted to evangelism. At my last service on the Sunday after the festival, we expected to reap the harvest of souls for the Kingdom of God. Many gave their lives to the Lord and many more of the packed congregation rededicated themselves to Jesus. It was an evening of great praise with the emphasis on looking forward, not back.

From now on I would receive no income from the Anglican Church. The Lord would truly be our Provider. The church family decided to donate the offering at that final service to the new ministry. But that was not the main encouragement from God that evening.

At the end of the service I was saying farewell to our dear friends at the church door, amid many hugs and tears. Among the crowd there was a little old lady with a shawl over her head. I could not ever recall seeing her before. She looked like the poor widow whom Jesus commended for placing her last coin in the Temple treasury.

As she shook my hand she pressed some crumpled paper into

my palm. "This is to encourage you," she said. And then she was gone, lost in the mêlée of bodies. I quickly stuffed the paper into my pocket to be ready for the next handshake or embrace.

I did not realise that it was money she had given me. Later I discovered that this dear old woman had placed one hundred and ten pounds cash in my hand. I was staggered. Was she just an old woman or was she an angel sent by God? Certainly the words she spoke rang in my heart. "This is to encourage you."

New Year's Day 1976 was cold and wintry. Soon we were to discover that the spiritual climate of our new area was equally cold and wintry; that we were moving from rich pastureland to a spiritual wilderness.

Two young people came with us, Vivienne de Pemberton and David Abbott. Both would spend some of their time travelling with me to assist in the leading of worship and Vivienne would also undertake the secretarial work. It was a small beginning, but we knew that our friends in Luton would be supporting us with much love and prayer.

We had allowed two or three weeks for settling down before beginning to travel and minister. During that period I returned to St. Albans to see the bishop. He gave me real encouragement for the future, while expressing a genuine concern about how we were going to survive financially. I could only reply that our trust was in the Lord, and we were confident that He would not allow us to starve. God had already assured us that this was His ministry and He would provide for it. If we had any need we were to ask Him, not men. We were not to contrive means of financial support or make any appeals for money: we simply had to trust Him.

At the time of speaking to the bishop I did not have much evidence to support our faith. But faith is not about evidence: "Now faith is being sure of what we hope for and certain of what we do not see" (Heb. 11:1). And faith is encouraged by knowing that God has spoken to your heart. If you believe what He has said, you have nothing to fear.

The bishop told me of the difficulties he was encountering

in finding a successor at St. Hugh's. All the people that I had
suggested to him at his request had been contacted, but without
success. They were men who were already seeing God's Spirit
moving in their churches and I could understand their reluctance
to move. I had experienced enough reluctance myself.

The conversation drifted onto a more personal note. "During
the past few years it seems that the Lord has asked of me one
impossible thing after another," I confided. "Things for which
I feel totally inadequate and incapable. And yet I have felt unable
to refuse Him. I know that this process is going to continue
and all I can do is to trust Him."

I could see the bishop looking very thoughtful. "It's as if
God has a calling on my life that is bigger than anything I can
handle," I continued. Was he identifying personally with what
I was saying?

His parting words were poignant: "Colin, if there is ever the
need, no matter where you are living, I want you to know that
I am ready to be a bishop to you."

2   From Revelation to Renewal

"I DISAGREE WITH absolutely everything you have said." The young minister moved swiftly onto the attack the moment I had finished my talk. For the next five minutes he poured out all his criticisms and objections to being baptised in the Holy Spirit, accusing me of saying several things that were the opposite of what I had actually said.

When he finished I suggested gently that he had listened to his own fears and preconceived ideas of what he thought I would say, a suggestion supported by grunts from several of the other ministers present. That young man was the first to be baptised in the Holy Spirit at that conference. Often, when under conviction, a person will almost violently oppose the truth, until he comes to a place of submission to the Lord's purposes.

Our new ministry began with this particular conference for ministers at Ashburnham Place, Sussex. During the next few years I was to speak at many gatherings for ministers. If local congregations were going to come alive in the power of the Holy Spirit, much would depend on the pastoral leadership given.

My first-hand experience of the problems and tensions, as well as the blessings, that were likely to arise in the process of seeing a fellowship transformed, was invaluable. I did not have to preach at these ministers (always a perilous occupation!), simply share what I had seen God do. That seemed to be a powerful witness. Clergy can argue their theological and doctrinal positions; it is far more difficult to question what God has actually done. People need revelation of what God wants to do in their lives, of what He wants to give them. Many dare not believe Him to give them anything. He is to be recognised, respected, worshipped, but it cannot be expected that He will intervene in the daily circumstances of life. Such lack of faith is expressed in a number of seemingly humble platitudes:

"Oh, I am not worthy to receive anything from God."
"He is much too busy to worry about poor little me."
"There are many others who are far worse off than I am."

I had encountered such attitudes countless times in recent years. I had also seen the wonder on people's faces as the Scriptures were opened up to them declaring the promises of God, showing the riches of the resources He makes available to us because of what He has already done through Jesus. To see that sense of wonder is as exciting as seeing people healed physically. Such revelation opens the way for God to change lives and establish His sovereignty in the hearts of those He is calling to be His children.

People need to receive revelation; the revelation that Jesus died to set us free from sin, fear and doubt. The revelation that He crucified us with Christ so that we might be dead to the old life of sin and self that separated us from God, and be raised to a new life as new creatures. The revelation that the power of the Holy Spirit is for Christians today, producing His fruit in their lives and making available the gifts of which the Scriptures speak so clearly. The revelation that God does not intend us to live our Christian lives in splendid isolation and independence; we are to belong to His Body, a people committed to one another in love. Revelation is the Holy Spirit bringing the Word of God to life in the hearts of people.

It is difficult to receive such revelation of the Good News without facing the bad news first. Without a personal coming to the cross of Jesus a man remains separated from God by his sins. Being a Christian is not a formal attending of church services, nor an attempt to be "good" people doing "good" works. It is not even a question of doing things *for* God, but rather allowing Him to do for us what we could never do for ourselves.

The act of new birth comes in response to faith in the Lord Jesus Christ. "Truly, truly, I say to you, he who hears my word and believes him who sent me, has eternal life; he does not come into judgment, but has passed from death to life." (John 5:24 R.S.V.)

At St. Hugh's it had been revelation for people to realise that they could pass from death to life *now*; that they could receive the gift of eternal life *now*; that they could know Jesus personally *now*; that their lives could be filled with His power, His love, joy and peace *now*; that He would bring His healing into lives *now*.

What was needed to enable such events to take place? Repentance. Each individual needed to turn his whole life over to God, seeking His forgiveness for the sin and failure of the past and allowing Him to give him new life, an entirely new beginning with His Spirit living within him. Experiences of the Holy Spirit without repentance would not result in fruitfulness.

Why should someone repent and turn his life over to God? Some do this in response to grave need in their lives, but a person does not have to wait for such a time before turning to the Lord. Repentance comes in response to revelation, God speaking to the heart of a man, penetrating the darkness of misunderstanding or spiritual ignorance.

Only pride and unbelief could prevent this turning to God once revelation had been received. As people came to the cross the way was cleared for God to meet with them in the power of His Holy Spirit.

Even for those who had been Christians for many years, a fresh and deeper repentance, or turning back to God, would lead to a fresh release of the power of the Holy Spirit in their lives. For some the Holy Spirit had been within but not allowed free expression. When speaking of the Holy Spirit, Jesus had said: "'Whoever believes in me, as the Scripture has said, streams of living water will flow from within him.' By this he

meant the Spirit, whom those who believed in him were later
to receive." (John 7:38–39)

Revelation needs to result in *repentance* which in turn leads to
personal renewal of individual Christian lives. That is only the
threshold of His true purpose. The release of the power of the
Holy Spirit in the lives of individual Christians simply empowers
them to be what God intends, a meaningful expression of the
Body of Christ, a people united in love, in mission and purpose.
Having received the life of Jesus, Christians have to learn how
to share and minister that life to one another and to the world
around. Then their corporate life will be a living testimony to
the presence of Jesus in the world, not simply by the words
they speak but by the people they are, the way they relate and
what they do.

Jesus prayed for all those who were to become His followers:
"May they be brought to complete unity to let the world know
that you sent me and have loved them even as you have loved
me." (John 17:23)

I had shared in the cost of aspiring to see such unity become
a reality. The flesh opposes the Spirit and people value their
independence and opinions. To be led in the way of the Spirit
is to be led in the way that the flesh does not want to go. That
is why the cross needs to be deeply imbedded in the lives of
all who really want to please and obey the Lord. "If anyone
would come after me, he must deny himself and take up his
cross and follow me. For whoever wants to save his life will
lose it, but whoever loses his life for me will find it."
(Matt. 16:24–25)

Anyone in a position of spiritual leadership must be prepared
to follow the Lord obediently in his personal life, for God will
ask him to lead people where they do not want to go as far as
their natural inclinations are concerned. And congregations can
be very vocal in expressing their opinions and desires.

There are relatively few denominational congregations which
manifest a marked renewal of their corporate life and worship.
Praise God for every one that does, and for the sensitive and

courageous leaders who are prepared to face the problems rather than be disobedient to the Lord.

Revelation, repentance, personal renewal, leading to corporate renewal. The Holy Spirit seems to work in this pattern which I have seen repeated in many parts of the world. In every situation it is worked out in a unique way; God does not have to copy in one place what He has done in another. Because it is the same Holy Spirit at work, it is hardly surprising that He should create the same quality of life wherever He is allowed freedom.

To be the Body of Christ in any locality, is to be reaching out to the lost and the needy with the life and power of Jesus, with His love and joy and peace, with His forgiveness and healing. As the Church of Jesus Christ we can only reach out with the resources that we ourselves have received and are leaning to share.

It was not long before I realised that many invitations I was receiving from ministers amounted to requests for me to come and renew their congregations for them. That was clearly impossible, because such a work can be done by the Holy Spirit alone. I could lead a time of ministry which would give revelation and bring people to repentance, which in turn would lead to personal renewal. But this was merely the prelude to the working out of the corporate life. That could be accomplished only by the Holy Spirit working through the leadership of that congregation.

People can go only where they are led. Individuals may receive great personal blessing from God but then find themselves utterly frustrated by the fact that nobody locally is prepared to lead them on in God's purposes. This is a widespread dilemma. In the mid 1970s many believed their leaders would take the opportunity of the changing spiritual climate, caused by the renewal, to exercise positive leadership in the power of the Holy Spirit. Certainly, there was intense interest among ministers from many different denominations and persuasions. The cost involved was apparent; there was no magic wand to be waved over a congregation to bring about instant renewal.

The cost begins with leading people to repentance and facing them with the need to seek God, to be built into a loving fellowship of believers relevant to the needs of the society in which they live. The cost continues with being prepared to share yourself, your resources, your needs, even your money with others according to the principles clearly stated in the New Testament. It is costly to open your home to needy people, to love the seemingly unlovable and to invite God to deal with you to make you more like Himself.

Some ministers and leaders have faced the cost. Others have sought personal renewal and blessing for themselves that has left the congregation virtually unaffected. Still others turn away. Why? In fear? Sometimes. For doctrinal reasons? Perhaps; but how sad that a man should not allow God to work in himself and others in the way He wants, simply because he cannot find the right doctrinal phrases to describe His activity.

It is tempting to think that still others are content to keep the denominational show going, to perpetuate the system, to please the congregation, hope for peace and a quiet retirement. That is said with sadness, not cynicism.

What a pressure there is on pastors! What genuine temptations beset them on every side! None can be stronger than the temptation to compromise one's ministry to make it acceptable to men. St. Paul said: "If I were still trying to please men, I would not be a servant of Christ." (Gal. 1:10)

Leadership involves sensitivity to the Holy Spirit. He gives the anointing that will encourage others to follow. Leadership includes setting the right example, not driving people. "Remember your leaders, who spoke the Word of God to you. Consider the outcome of their way of life and imitate their faith." (Heb. 13:7)

Sharing with ministers this vision of what a local church can become in the power of the Holy Spirit, was one side of the ministry. The other was the public meetings, conference sessions and rallies.

The Sunday evening service at St. Hugh's had attracted many

people from beyond the parish and from every imaginable back-ground: Catholic nuns, Pentecostals, Baptists, Methodists, folk from Brethren Assemblies, the Salvation Army, and so on. Every week there was a unity service in the power of the Spirit, at which people came to know the Lord Jesus, were baptised in the Holy Spirit and healed without having specific "altar-calls" or "invitations". Those visiting would come among a body of praising people who were sharing their lives in love, were used to praying with others, and among whom the power of God had been liberated. Very rarely did I lay hands on people or minister personally to them at those services.

When travelling I did not have such a ministering body of people. More expectancy was directed towards me personally. I resisted that with all my might. People's expectancy needed to be in the Lord; it was to Him they should be looking, not me. And I believed fundamentally in the ministry of the Body, without emphasis upon any individual or personality. In time God was to modify these views. He showed me that the Scrip-tures are the revelation of God working through particular personalities. He will not work through those motivated by pride; He promises to bring them low. The more broken and humbled a man is before God, the more God can use him, whether in a non-spectacular role as a faithful servant and witness, or in a more public ministry of evangelism and healing.

It was my responsibility to lead people to the throne of God's grace, to meaningful repentance, before praying for them to be filled with the Holy Spirit or receive healing. In doing this I needed to be humble before God and men.

My whole life became a preparation to ensure that the Lord would speak and act through me. There needed to be a prophetic element in what I was saying; I needed to give the specific message that God wanted for those people in that place at that time. Time must be spent waiting on the Lord, developing that spiritual ear to hear and know His voice.

Sometimes He would lay a particular message on my heart to be spoken in one situation after another, but there would always be differences in detail and presentation. It was essential to be "in the Spirit" when speaking; I had to be in the right place with God so that He could speak through me. The message had to come from my heart and I had an agreement with God that I would not speak what I was not attempting to live out myself. There could be no room for spiritual theory.

It was also essential to hear clearly the leading of the Holy Spirit during the time of ministry following the proclamation of the Word. If God has spoken to His people there needs to be an opportunity for them to respond to what He has said. This part of the meeting was not to be hurried. God will work among His people if only He is given the time to do so.

At most meetings there are those who do not know Jesus and need to be brought into a personal relationship with Him; those who need the power of the Holy Spirit to be released in their lives and others who need to receive healing from God, or some specific answer to prayer. There will be specific things arising from the sermon which must be met with a positive response, even if obedience to what the Lord is saying can only be fulfilled subsequent to the meeting. He is concerned with faithful obedience in our daily lives, rather than acts of commitment or statements of intent.

If Jesus is truly present among His people, things will be happening to them. Some of these events may be spectacular; most will be happening quietly in people's hearts. Many need to be shown how to repent and come to the Lord Jesus. They can be taken through various areas of sin, failure and dis-obedience, laying them before the Lord and asking for His forgiveness, talking to Jesus from their hearts as if He stood in front of them. He is the one who casts out fear by His perfect love and who can dispel doubt. "All that is not of faith is sin." Fear is certainly not of faith, neither is doubt. A person may need to be set free from the effects of fear in his life, but he still needs to confess the sin of the fear itself.

True and full repentance involves more than asking God to deal with the negative areas of our lives. It involves also a handing over of the positive aspects of all that we are and have. Jesus is to be Lord of our families, relationships, time, work, leisure, our participation in the local congregation. He is to be Lord of our money and property, so that everything is at His disposal to be used for His glory.

The initial act of repentance that leads to new birth, should be thorough. The new Christian needs to understand that he is not joining some religious society or social club, but is committing himself to a way of life that involves every aspect of his being. Christianity is all or nothing. That is not a truth for the spiritually elite, but God's calling upon every Christian life. So mature Christians need to reaffirm constantly that their lives belong to God, that He is their Lord and Sovereign.

Having turned to Him in repentance, people need assurance of God's forgiveness, acceptance and love, whether they are new Christians or have been serving Him for years. What a great gift it is to receive the peace that is beyond understanding, when you know that God has forgiven you, that He has washed away your sins, your failure and disobedience through the cleansing power of His blood! Together with that peace can come faith and confidence that God will also answer need. The greatest need is to know the vitality of His Holy Spirit surging through our lives, enabling us to live in dependence on Him.

Many who have been baptised in the Holy Spirit are only too aware that the rivers of God's living water are not flowing out from them in the way God intends — the rivers of love, joy, peace, power, forgiveness, healing etc.

Such is the hunger in people's hearts and their ready response to the Word of God that it is common for hundreds to be seeking this gift. The laying on of hands is often helpful in encouraging people to believe that they are receiving at that moment what they are asking of Him. Such an act is not *necessary* and God can touch lives without that physical act of an intermediary. The Lord means what he promises: "Ask and it will be given to you ... For everyone who asks receives ... how much more will your Father in heaven give the Holy Spirit to those who ask Him." (Luke 11:9,10,12)

Some may doubt that God has honoured His Word; they have been looking for some particular emotional experience, or external evidence, or spiritual gift to convince them that they have received from God. He wants us to approach Him with faith. When people believe that they have received from God what He has promised to give, then they are able to experience His gifts. Faith precedes the gift; the gift does not precede faith.

Healing is part of the ministry of the Holy Spirit. It is an advantage to administer this gift in a pastoral setting when it is possible to minister to the whole person, body, soul and spirit—not simply the specific need that has been identified. The sick person can be led to a full repentance (except in cases of extremity, mental instability, or with very young children). The one ministering can ensure that there is faith to believe God to work. With repentance and faith, there can be every confidence that the prayer for healing will result in God's power being manifested. Although healing has been restored to the life of the Church in several places, there are still many who do not have such ministry available to them in their local congregation.

The corporate faith of believers joined in worship releases the power of God in ways not always experienced in personal ministry. Healing is the sovereign work of God, and during the past six years I have seen thousands healed from a great variety of diseases, healings that have stood the test of time.

Some object that not all are healed at such meetings. Surely we cannot criticise God for healing? Neither can we judge Him for not healing everyone. Nor can we say to God: "You are to heal everyone or nobody at all!" He is Lord, He is sovereign in His dealings with men. He has never made a mistake and gives men "their food at the proper time." (Ps. 145:15)

Some of the healings I have received have been immediate answers to prayer; for others I have had to wait months and sometimes years. I bow before the wisdom of God in knowing best how and when to release the healing that I have been seeking. It is important to respect what Jesus teaches about perseverance in prayer, not giving up because there does not appear to be an immediate response from Him.

If I had my way, every sick or crippled person would be

healed at every meeting. I would rejoice for those needy people, wouldn't you? We all have to acknowledge that it is God's way that matters, not ours. He encourages faith to believe Him to act in sovereign and miraculous ways; but He is always right in the way in which He deals with every one of us.

The pattern of ministry evolved quickly as I began to lead large services and renewal meetings: the proclaiming of the Word, a time of repentance with the assurance of God's forgiveness, prayer for people to be baptised in the Holy Spirit, followed by the ministry of healing. Patterns can be useful if they are well tested by experience and are clearly used by God. They must never become rigid systems if we are seeking to follow the leading of the Holy Spirit. At any time, He can lead in a different way, and cause a different sequence of events — and we must always be open to that.

My need was to be in that place with God which allowed Him to speak through me in the way that He desired, and to follow the leading of His Spirit in the time of ministry. Hearing Him was not enough; boldness was needed to do what He said. That boldness would need to increase in succeeding years.

3 My Constant Companion

"LORD, WE DON'T have the money!" It sounded a lame protest. The new ministry was only three months old and Vivienne, David and I had just returned from Scotland. We had to travel long distances regularly and arrive on time for meetings. Clearly we needed to have a reliable car and our present one had already covered a high mileage.

God had provided for our needs and we had kept to our agreement with Him not to ask men for anything — even expenses. If we were asked "What are your expenses?" our reply was: "Nothing." This often produced reactions of surprise, or even annoyance, from treasurers until we explained.

At that time there were a few hundred pounds in the bank account; enough, together with the trade-in value of our present car, to buy a reasonable second-hand one. We prayed and asked the Lord to lead us to such a car. David and I then went to visit local showrooms.

At the first we found the car we were looking for; one previous owner, low mileage, good condition. The dealer offered us a surprisingly high price for the present car, and was eager to clinch the deal. I felt it right to talk to the others first and seek assurance from the Lord that this was the car He intended for us.

As we all prayed together, I realised that He was saying something I did not want to hear. "I have led you to the kind of car you asked for, a good second-hand car. With the mileage you cover, you would need to replace that within a few months. You are to go out and buy a new car."

Hence my response, "Lord, we don't have the money." A battle raged inside me. God answered my objections by saying that He had plenty of money. He had promised to supply every need and we were to trust Him to do that. He repeated the command: "Go out and buy a new car."

I had heard of other people acting in such foolish ways, buying things without having the money. It had always seemed a perilous course of action and would be dishonouring to the Lord if not initiated by Him. I was only too aware of the pitfalls ahead if I was not hearing Him correctly.

The others agreed that God wanted us to exercise faith for a new car. It was clearly going to be a lesson in faith to trust Him for the additional money that would be required.

We settled on a particular model and sat down with the dealer to complete the paper-work. "The car will be ready for collection in one week," he said. I sighed with relief. At least the Lord would have a whole seven days in which to supply. Even if we were to empty our bank account completely, we would still require over six hundred pounds, a sum worth rather more then than now.

"How will you be paying the difference, by cash or hire-purchase?" The salesman looked at me enquiringly. I faltered.

"By cash; well, we may need hire-purchase for some of it." Oh the lack of faith! It has not occurred to me beforehand to enter into a hire-purchase agreement; I didn't like the idea in principle. The salesman filled out the necessary application form. I felt distinctly uneasy, but comforted myself with the thought that we could withdraw the application if, or when, the money was supplied by the Lord.

David and I returned home and told the others to pray. Surely, our agreement with the Lord not to ask men for money included hire-purchase agreements! I had to repent of that application and somehow knew that it would not be needed.

On the following day the money began to arrive. There were a number of gifts of varying amounts, many of them from people we did not know personally. Several were accompanied by letters which included such phrases as: "The Lord has told me to send you this ..." It was a great comfort to know that we were on His mailing list.

On the day before we were due to collect the new car, a registered envelope arrived containing several twenty-pound notes. The amount took us past the required figure. We were overjoyed, not so much at the prospect of having a new car, nor with the money itself, but with the faithfulness and love the Lord had shown us, despite all our hesitancy and doubt. I was able to telephone the dealer and tell him that hire-purchase would not be required.

The post arrived before we left to collect the car on the following morning. One envelope enclosed a further gift together with a slip of paper on which was written: "This is the day that the Lord will provide." The wonderful workings of our God! This gift meant that our bank account would not be completely empty.

However, I was soon to go on my first tour of ministry abroad — almost seven weeks in Australia and New Zealand. We would receive some gifts from the few engagements I had before leaving; but then there would be no definite income all the time I was away. I felt a responsibility towards my family and household and laid the matter before the Lord.

One of my last engagements was an evening rally at Tunbridge Wells. It was a night of great blessing as the Lord moved powerfully among His people. After the meeting one of the leaders told me that a gift would be sent for our ministry. When the cheque arrived soon before my departure, we were staggered to see that the offering had amounted to well over six hundred pounds. All that for one evening of ministry! We were learning that God knows our need and supplies accordingly; He does not pay us for doing a job. We have learned to rejoice no matter what is given, for God oversees our finances; it is not for us to tell Him how to provide.

With that sum of money in the bank I could go away with

a peaceful mind, knowing that those at home were well provided for financially.

The same could not be said about spiritual provision for the family. At the time of leaving Luton our three children were still young. Claire was ten and had enjoyed a personal relationship with Jesus for about four years; Clive was eight and very aware of spiritual things; Andrea was nearly six and had been praising the Lord in tongues since she was three. They were accustomed to worship that was full of life, love and joy.

When we moved, it was natural for us to become part of the local Anglican church. After our experience at St. Hugh's it was a shock to discover that there were no fellowship groups, prayer meetings or healing ministry; no evangelism or outreach, no teaching, nothing except the Sunday services. Instead of a full church there were only a few dozen people scattered around the building.

Our children were full of questions:

"Why is everybody so sad?"

"Why don't all these people love Jesus?"

"Why is it so boring?"

"Do we have to go?" A question that did not arise in Luton!

Most weekends I was away ministering in other places, often with Vivienne and David. We could experience plenty of worship in the Spirit during the course of our ministry. But Caroline and the children were at home week in and week out. My concern was for their spiritual welfare. It was difficult not to be negative in our attitudes towards this new situation.

Every time I worshipped at home it gave me encouragement to devote myself to the renewal of the Church. It made me appreciate the position of so many who were being baptised in the Spirit throughout the country, and who were worshipping in similar situations. That gave an added sensitivity to the nature of the problems underlying questions I was often asked. "Should I stay in my present church, even though the gospel isn't preached and there is no openness to the ministry of the Holy Spirit?" "How can I submit to the authority of a minister who

is not born again?" "My minister forbids speaking in tongues
in our church. He is going against the Scriptures in saying that.
What can I do about it?"

Many people believed it right to stay in those congregations
and use every opportunity to witness and share the life of Jesus
with others. It would not be a very good witness if everyone
who was baptised in the Holy Spirit immediately left his church.
Congregations would never become renewed in that way. A witness of love needed to be given within every fellowship. Those who
had discovered a new spiritual vitality were to be leaven in the lump.

At the same time, there were those who were saying that such
a policy would be useless and fruitless. The old wine skins could
not contain the new wine. Better to leave the historic denominations and join new house fellowships, which would be un-
cluttered by tradition and outmoded structure.

The ministry God had called me to fulfil was aimed at encouraging local churches to become what they should be:
meaningful expressions of the Body of Christ. And yet, by no
stretch of the imagination could it be said that our local church
even aspired to such a purpose.

The Lord dealt with our negative and critical attitudes. His
presence was within us, so we could worship Him no matter
how lifeless the service may seem. There was no purpose in
being critical in the lack of gospel content in the preaching either.
If we went to a service expecting to hear the Lord, we would
hear Him. From the time God ministered that to us, I heard
the Lord speak to me through every sermon.

But the agony of having to make children go to church when
worship should be a joyful and exciting experience! And how difficult, having tested the reality of Spirit-led worship, to be
plunged into the dryness of formal services. I was thankful for
the devotional life they could enjoy in our home.

It was not only vitality in worship that was missing, but genuine
fellowship — the sharing of our lives together in Jesus. Even in
the home that was only a spasmodic thing for Caroline, as
Vivienne, David and I were so often away. We would have liked
a larger household, but there was no further room in the house.

God had taught Caroline that He was her husband and she learned to cling to her relationship with Him. Despite the lack of fellowship, she continued to grow spiritually and to look to Him directly.

When planning my itinerary, I did not appreciate sufficiently the time that would be spent in travelling, nor the physical pressure involved; what would be required in prayer and preparation. A couple of days between trips to be with the family seemed reasonable. But when I returned home exhausted, there would always be a pile of letters to answer, telephone calls to respond to, articles to be written and the next unfinished book already late for the publisher's deadline — not to mention the need to prepare for the next trip and the pile of invitations to be considered. It was so difficult to decline the pleas for help; opportunities to encourage renewal in the Church were not to be missed.

Cecil Marshall, director of Christian Advance Ministries, had invited me to tour New Zealand, speaking at a series of conferences, renewal gatherings and ministers' seminars. This would cover a four-week period, followed by two weeks in Australia.

At first I felt it right in principle that I should not travel alone. Renewal is a corporate expression of life, and Jesus sent the disciples out two by two. I would need someone to be in fellowship with and to pray with. However, I sensed that God was telling me to go alone this time, as He needed to do a work of healing in my life.

By nature, I was a shy and diffident person. When young, I was always the quiet one who sat in a corner and said nothing at meetings. I had a fear of anyone in authority. Feeling unacceptable, I found it difficult to make relationships with people. God had dealt with this problem to a great extent while at St. Hugh's. There it was possible to enter into loving relationships with others and allow myself to be loved in return. It was one thing to make relationships in a static situation with people you knew and to whom you could relate over a prolonged period of time. It was another matter to relate to people I didn't know, and with whom I would be staying for only a brief time.

On this trip, I was to look to the Lord and see Him enabling relationships with other people. The prospect was daunting, as anyone with an over-sized inferiority complex will know. Once again, God was giving me faith for the future by His assurance of His personal companionship and the healing that would result.

I felt very lonely after I had said goodbye to Caroline, the children, Vivienne and David at Heathrow Airport. This was the first of many such partings; but none has been more lonely than that first one. Any excitement there might have been about flying off to the other side of the world, via such places as India and Hong Kong, was far outweighed by the personal crisis of feeling alone except, that is, for the Lord.

As I boarded the plane, I was hoping desperately that I would not have to talk much to the person sitting next to me for over thirty hours. Mercifully, the seat was empty! The Lord was dealing with me gently.

My inexperience in planning an itinerary showed immediately; I was speaking on the evening of my arrival in Dunedin. As I stood to speak the whole hall was swaying from side to side. I had to cling to the lectern to keep my balance.

During my time in New Zealand, submission, authority and leadership were the main themes of the teaching. To be speaking in that vein continuously for four weeks was heavy going; but many came to a new freedom in the Spirit as they submitted themselves to God in a more meaningful way than before.

Cecil Marshall, my host and a lovely man of God, introduced me as "the gentle clobberer". "He speaks gently and lovingly," Cecil would say, "while hitting you over the head with a spiritual four-by-two!"

Renewal had already progressed considerably in New Zealand by 1976. Many had been baptised in the Spirit and the country was renowned for the flow of new gospel songs that were the product of the renewal. The problems were similar to those being experienced in England. Many individuals were being blessed, but still relatively few congregations showed a marked renewal of their corporate life.

While I was leading a mission in the parish of Tawa, near Wellington, the national television company filmed a fifteen-minute interview, together with part of the Ascension Day Eucharist at which I was ministering. The broadcast on Pentecost Sunday included the time of leading people in repentance. In the front row was a burly man who broke down in tears as he came to the Lord and received the gift of eternal life. The prayer, together with this powerful visual aid, came over with startling simplicity.

The secret of the Lord's power in our lives and ministries lies in our submission to His authority. This was the substance of the teaching at a ministers' conference. At the end of the final service all the delegates danced around the communion table, full of the Lord's joy. Then they gathered round me to pray for my family at home and later wrote a corporate letter to Caroline to express their appreciation for her allowing her husband to come to New Zealand.

Over the years we have known many touching actions of love like that. They are a great encouragement to Caroline and the children and help them feel part of the ministry, even when I am thousands of miles away.

When you are overseas, people don't want to waste your time while you are with them; so they fill it! It is normal to receive an outline itinerary for approval a few weeks before travelling, but usually before departure another letter arrives, with a revised itinerary. Because of the number of requests, it has seemed right to include additional meetings! The national organiser has to leave local arrangements to a local committee. When you arrive in that locality, you discover that further meetings have been arranged. To decline to fulfil any of them would be ungracious. It is impossible to understand the pressures of a travelling ministry without experiencing them personally. The message you are proclaiming is often a challenging one, and you have to see people through their reactions and the conflicts they experience as they face up to what God is speaking to their hearts.

It is not only the actual talks and times of ministry that are demanding, both mentally and physically; there are all the conversations in between. From the start of the day until the late evening there is talk, talk, talk; the kind of talk that involves deep concentration.

I had found such ministry demanding in Britain; but it was possible to have a break from its intensity every few days. Now I was going from one place to another, to a never-ending series of meetings and new relationships. As soon as I had seen one set of people make a spiritual breakthrough, then I was on yet another jet to a new place, not even knowing who was going to meet me at the airport, and having to be ready to start all over again.

The Lord was certainly teaching me what it meant for Him to be my companion in all this. Cecil Marshall knew the demands of such ministry and had arranged for a brief respite in a mountain chalet mid-way through the tour. The mountain air and some good walks would be a good change from sitting and standing in meeting places and aeroplanes.

As we approached our destination it began to rain heavily. I never saw the mountain. In fact it required an act of faith to believe there was a mountain! It rained all night, all the next day, the following night and the morning after, when it was time to leave for the next conference. In this the Lord was sovereign, for all I could do was rest — and build relationships with the team from Christian Advance Ministries.

There were a further two weeks of ministry and travelling in New Zealand before I bade farewell to that beautiful country. I had now been away for over four weeks, a time of constant talking, and I was ready for home. But first there was Australia!

There are a great many similarities between life in New Zealand and Britain. There were also many similarities in the way the renewal was developing in both countries. I soon found Australia to be very different. Society there seemed harder and more brash than New Zealand, and the pace of life faster. Renewal had begun slowly but was gaining momentum.

Many countries were experiencing renewal in the early 1970s, and nearly all the Pentecostal churches were suspicious of what was now happening in the historic denominations; in some places they stood right apart from the renewal. Australia was different. There the renewal had begun through the direct influence of Pentecostals. Evidence of this could be seen in the worship which had a distinctly American Pentecostal flavour about it. To me it seemed noisier and more superficial than the worship in the Spirit to which I was accustomed, and I found it difficult at first.

It was strange to see Methodists, Anglicans and Catholics trying to behave like Pentecostals. The Holy Spirit will always give us His style of worship, appropriate to each group, without having to copy the way He works through others.

Those first days in Australia were difficult for me. I arrived from New Zealand very tired, had no time to acclimatise, had to become used to a very different society and start learning about this new situation.

I was grateful for Alan Langstaff's friendship. As director of Temple Trust, he was a central figure in the renewal in Australia. It was a great joy to have fellowship with key men whom God has chosen to use in these times.

Harry Westcott was another in this category. Immediate friendship developed between Harry and Doreen, his English-born wife, and myself. He was then the minister of O'Connor Methodist Church in Canberra. Here was a congregation really concerned to move on with God. It was like ministering at St. Hugh's several years before, when the Spirit was beginning to move powerfully there.

The visit to Australia was brief and I could gain only a glimpse of the exciting things that were beginning to stir. But it was with relief that I boarded the plane for England. On this trip, I had already made over twenty flights and had spoken at over eighty meetings. I was longing to be home and I resolved never to have such a long and intensive time of ministry again. Perhaps Australia was not my scene. Then the Lord spoke clearly to me and said that I would be returning often to Australia as He had a particular purpose for me there.

Inwardly I groaned; I was in no mood for more! Yielding to what He says is sometimes an act of the will. Little did I realise the profound affect my next visit was to have on my life.

4   A Warning from God

"YOUR VOICE MUST be heard among the nations . . ." The visit to New Zealand and Australia was the beginning of the fulfilment of what God had said nearly six years before.

However, the bulk of my ministry would still be in Britain and I had a great desire to see renewal in all the churches of my own land. In 1976 the scene here was both varied and encouraging — as was the ministry. One day I could be speaking to a small group of people earnestly seeking the Lord for renewal in their local congregation. The next I could be addressing a large crowd packed into a cathedral or conference centre. God's people were hungry.

When the Spirit Comes told of the development of the work at St. Hugh's. God had used that little book to whet spiritual appetites. There must be more to the spiritual life than going to church on Sundays, making a very poor attempt at contacting God in prayer, and trying to understand the Bible. Every meeting was a wonderful evangelistic opportunity and the response of people to the Lord was encouraging. Many were coming into a living personal relationship with Him and were experiencing the power of the Holy Spirit in a real way for the first time.

However, I missed seeing people through their problems and needs, watching the transformation that took place in them when they surrendered their lives to Jesus. In this travelling ministry people were led to the Lord, but I could not see the fruit that resulted.

I had to be content with the knowledge that God had met with His people and had been at work among them. Letters giving testimony of God's specific activity were good to receive as confirmation of what He was doing.

In September I spent a few days in Ohio, my first visit to the U.S.A. Some Christians there had read *When the Spirit Comes* and invited me to a series of meetings as a prelude to a time of ministry in Canada.

In Toronto I was the guest speaker at the Anglican Diocesan Renewal Conference. The bishop had appointed a renewal committee to encourage and oversee spiritual renewal in the diocese. Some 300 attended the conference, after which I spoke at various centres in the diocese. The bishop presided at a day conference for his clergy, at which the Spirit of God moved in a beautiful way.

That morning I experienced violent physical pain; I couldn't sit or keep still, but had to walk around outside while people were assembling. My trust had to lie in the Lord as I prayed constantly in tongues. Once I started ministering the pain would go, as the Spirit took complete control of events. This was not the first time that I had suffered such an attack; they always seemed to come before God was about to do something really important.

I experienced a difficulty of a different kind a few days later. We had travelled north and seen the beautiful colouring of the Ontario trees in October. While ministering I am deeply immersed in what I am doing. It is in the few times of relaxation that I greatly miss my wife, my family and loved ones. I wished they were with me to enjoy this time together. Although I had enjoyed the magnificent scenery, I felt emotionally unsettled and found it hard to concentrate when preparing for the evening meeting. I could only trust that the Holy Spirit would provide the words to speak.

God can redeem every situation. I became deeply aware of His presence, spoke very simply about His love and the Lord moved graciously among His people. When I revisited the same town on a subsequent tour of Ontario, I heard that people had taken the blessing of God's love back to their congregations to share with others and several churches were now being renewed.

From the province of Ontario, I flew to Victoria on Vancouver Island. The Lord had used John Vickers to begin a Renewal Centre there. He was a retired priest, a gracious and loving man who despite his advanced years was to be used to encourage renewal throughout Canada, a tremendous task in view of the size of that country.

For several days I made a tour of the main centres of the diocese and also a brief visit to the remote northern part of the Island. This required being flown in a single-engined mission plane, to the other side of the range of mountains that divide the Island into two distant areas. The altitude at which such an aircraft can fly is restricted; we had to fly through a pass, rather than over the top of the mountains. After take-off the weather closed in and the clouds descended. We flew parallel to the mountains for a while, but there was no sign of a way through. There was only one answer: pray.

As we prayed the clouds suddenly parted at the point of the very pass we wanted. We flew straight through. As we looked behind us, the clouds had come together again! The Lord hears the prayers of His children, and He wanted to encourage the thirty people who gathered for the meeting from remote settlements.

Continually for two weeks, I had spoken at different places. Although the Lord uses these "one-night stands", it can be frustrating to speak to an entirely different set of people day after day. It is far more satisfying, from my point of view, to speak to the same group for several days. I sensed that a longer time in each place would prove more fruitful. It was good, therefore, that my time in Canada finished with a four-day mission in Victoria. The response of the people there must have caused all heaven to rejoice and I was made aware of His love through others, always a great blessing in this travelling ministry.

People come to meetings expecting to hear from God, expecting to meet with Him; some come expecting specific healing in their lives. Expectancy is essential, but must be centred on the Lord: He can withstand the pressure.

In this travelling ministry considerable mental pressure existed, not so much as a result of people's expectations but through being aware of my responsibility to the Lord. He wanted to speak through me. I had to lead people to the cross and to His throne of grace. I had to be in the right place spiritually so I could hear His voice and be used of Him. The degree of concentration required was high and I was conscious of how spiritually intense my life was becoming.

Added to this was the fact that our programme had been grossly overfilled. As I came to the end of the first year of travelling, I was beginning to feel exhausted; not a superficial tiredness, but a deep inner exhaustion.

In November I led a houseparty for students from Bristol University. At the beginning of the weekend it was apparent how exhausted I was. Frankly, I was wondering how I would get through the full programme that lay ahead of me that weekend — not to mention coping with yet more new relationships.

With love and great sensitivity the students spent some time ministering to me, and the Lord spoke prophetically to encourage me. When I began to speak I started to feel refreshed. The more I ministered, the better I felt. Caroline was expecting the usual exhausted Colin to return home; instead she was amazed and delighted to have a revitalised husband.

The Lord taught me something very important in this. I had to have the right mental attitude as well as the right spiritual attitude. Spiritually I knew that the Lord would sustain me, speak through me, use me for His glory. If mentally I expected to be exhausted and worn out as a result, then that is how I would be. But if I had a positive attitude that I was not going to be overcome with weariness, then I would not fall into a negative reaction that would ultimately lead to self-pity — one of the most destructive reactions that can take place in any human being.

So the first year of an itinerant ministry drew to a close. It had been a busy time but one in which I had learned much and had known the Lord dealing constantly with me. The fruit of the ministry was an indication that it had certainly been the right decision to leave parish life. The one cloud hanging over my life was the news filtering through about St. Hugh's. "The place has lost its anointing" seemed to be the verdict of many who had visited recently.

Caroline, Vivienne and David chose their moments very carefully if there was something to communicate about our former parish; they knew how sensitive I was on the subject because of my love for the people and my gratitude to the Lord for all that He had done there.

During the last six months of my time in Luton, I had withdrawn from the leadership group to enable the others to become used to seeking the Lord for His direction, without depending on me in any way. I could be consulted or step in with advice, which was hardly ever necessary.

After my departure, the news had been encouraging at first. The other leaders were giving good support to Trevor Blackshaw, the curate. Then how could such a work lose its anointing so rapidly? I was perplexed. Whenever I talked to people from the parish I received a series of defensive and self-justifying statements, which seemed to indicate that what I was hearing from others was true.

As I sought to understand the situation, it became clear that although as individuals the people loved the Lord, their corporate commitment to one another, which had been so costly and had produced such fruit, was beginning to diminish. As a result the worship began to suffer and it became apparent to others that there was not the same anointing upon the people.

I was constantly being asked, "What is happening at St. Hugh's now?" Increasingly, that was an embarrassing and difficult question to answer. However, I resolved always to be positive in my response.

It was left to small groups of people to work out their commitment in community. The demands for ministry from both beyond the parish and within were less than they used to be, and one by one the six full-time lay workers went back to secular employment. The leadership group was disbanded. What had

taken years to build was being taken apart. I could no longer
say to people: "Go and see what is happening there." I would
be happier if they didn't.

All this would have been exceedingly difficult to bear if God
had not prepared me for it before leaving St. Hugh's. He warned
me that the sun was going to set on the place and there would
follow a dark night. There was nothing that I could do to prevent
this. It would not be right for me to stay and try to haul the
sun back into the sky. Night was coming, but beyond every night
there is the hope of a new dawn. I did not dare to tell anyone
except Caroline about this word from the Lord; I did not want
to leave the people with a negative, defeated attitude.

Not that St. Hugh's should have continued as it was when
I was there. In the early seventies there were only a few churches
in this country that demonstrated any appreciable amount of
corporate renewal. Each one had become a centre of ministry
in the Holy Spirit. Now there was not quite the same need as
more fellowships were openly moving in the things of the Spirit.

The anointing of the Holy Spirit upon the corporate life of
any fellowship depends upon corporate obedience, a willingness
to move on with God. There needs to be a ready repentance
in the hearts of His people, something that is incompatible with
defensiveness and self-justification. There will be those who
stubbornly refuse to repent or move on in obedience. In Scripture that is rebellion, a most serious offence against the Lord.
Where rebellion is allowed to influence and manipulate the
situation, there cannot be the anointing that God desires to see
upon His people.

If the news from St. Hugh's caused increasing concern, there
was relief in another direction at the end of 1976. My second
book *My Father is the Gardener*, was finally finished. I had begun
to write this in Luton and hoped to finish it before leaving there.
That proved impossible. My programme had been so busy since
that it was extremely difficult to finish the manuscript. The book
had begun as a commentary on John 15:1–17. There Jesus speaks
many encouraging words to His disciples, but He also challenges
them. In particular He warns that fruitless branches are cut from

the True Vine by His Father; and that every fruitful branch will be pruned to make it more fruitful. He gives them the new commandment to love one another as He has loved them — and that means laying down their lives for one another.

When I finished the first draft, my reaction was: "People won't be able to take it." God had led us step by step into these things. What was now happening at St. Hugh's supported the fact that it was not easy to face the cost (and maintain that) if the corporate life of a fellowship was to be what God intended. How could the teaching be given in such a way that people would be able to relate personally to what Jesus was saying?

After praying about this, I decided to rewrite the book, giving the teaching through fictitious characters in a fictitious situation. To some people this made it a novel, although my intention was that it should be a teaching book, but with the teaching put in a readable and receivable style. I know from personal experience how difficult it is to read "heavy" books. Many people put them to one side and do not persevere with them. It is always my purpose to be simple and direct when either speaking or writing. If God is going to speak to ordinary folks like myself, He is going to use direct and easily understood methods.

My Father is the Gardener is about the personal and corporate problems that need to be faced if churches are to be renewed in the Holy Spirit. People often ask if the characters are based on real individuals. They are not, but the characters and the situations that face them are all based on experience of people and how they relate. Readers often see themselves in one or more of the characters and that is the intention. For the book is not about living individuals, but people, and the problems they have as they face the Lord's purposes in their lives.

Were the years at St. Hugh's invalidated by what happened afterwards? I do not believe so. There are many lovely people in that parish who know and love the Lord as a result of meeting with Him there. Many hundreds of people from other places also came to know the Lord there or met with Him in life-transforming encounters. *When the Spirit Comes* and *My Father is the Gardener* were written as a direct result of my ministry there. And God has chosen to use what could only be described as loaves and fishes, to feed a multitude.

Also, those years were formative for me and for others whom the Lord has led away from Luton to fruitful areas of ministry elsewhere. He is the Lord who anoints, builds and uses what is His to use in the ways that He desires, and for as long as He chooses. And that is a warning to all of us. No matter how much the Lord has done in our lives in the past, we have to remain faithful and obedient to Him if we are to increase in fruitfulness. In the Christian life there are two alternatives: to go on, or to go back.

5 Spiritual Hunger

"THE ONLY PLACE where people are not sitting," the archbishop said, "is on the Holy Table itself!"

The cathedral in Cape Town, South Africa, was packed for the third night of the mission on an extremely hot January evening. On the first evening every seat had been taken by the multiracial congregation. On the second, the floor as well as the seats was filled with praising people. For this third meeting every available space was taken. On the following evening, the archbishop and I found it difficult to get into the building ourselves although we arrived half an hour before the service was due to begin. We were stepping over bodies to get to the front. People were standing on the steps and in the streets outside unable to get in. When the dean arrived shortly before the service was due to begin, he took one look at the situation and drove away again. He had been unable to get into his own cathedral!

There were great spiritual stirrings in South Africa. I was there at the invitation of Bill Burnett, the Archbishop of Cape Town, for two weeks of ministry in his diocese, and would then be travelling to other cities in the republic. My initial reaction to the invitation had been: "Lord, what good could I possibly do in South Africa? I don't understand the situation there." God took no notice of my objections.

A short time before my visit, there had been a series of riots in some of the black townships which had brought South Africa into the international headlines once again. Yet despite, or perhaps because of, the political situation there, the Holy Spirit was moving in powerful ways.

I was expecting to learn a great deal from this visit; it would be fatal to prejudge the situation. The Lord had sent me to minister to the needs of His people, individually and corporately as His body. There would be no purpose in making political or anti-government statements. If I did so I would be put on the next London-bound jet. The political statements needed to be made by those involved in the situation, not by outsiders like myself. The spiritual answer to apartheid is to bring the love of God and the unity of His Spirit into the lives of His people. And that is what I saw happening in those great services in Cape Town Cathedral.

It is incredibly difficult to describe meetings in which the Spirit of God moves in sovereign ways. The lives of a great many people were touched in those days and there was much reconciliation between those of different races, as their hearts were touched by the Spirit of God's love. It was a moving sight to see people of different races embracing each other as they shared the peace of Jesus with one another. I stood there amazed at the power of God's love and the way in which the Spirit can break down barriers that have existed for years.

Even the journey to South Africa had shown that this was to be a trip in which I was to see God move in sovereign ways. The flight was delayed for some time at Heathrow Airport and again at Paris. We were several hours behind schedule. I would miss my connecting flight for Cape Town at Johannesburg. Unless, of course, God intervened.

The pilot apologised for the delay and said that it would be impossible to make up the lost time as there would be a strong headwind throughout the journey.

"Lord, I don't believe you want me to miss that connecting flight and cause inconvenience to the folk in Cape Town. Please enable the plane to arrive in Johannesburg in time to catch the other flight." I had peace that the whole matter was in His hands and settled down to sleep.

The pilot spoke to us at breakfast time: "It is remarkable.

Somehow we have managed to make up one and a half hours despite having the headwind. I cannot understand." He didn't add "Hallelujah"; I did that for him.

I caught the connecting flight in good time and was met at Cape Town airport by Sheila Burnett, the archbishop's wife. I was glad she had not been kept waiting.

What a tremendous difference it makes to a diocese to be led by a man baptised in the Holy Spirit. The testimony of how the Lord met with Bill Burnett while he was Bishop of Grahamstown is widely known. Most of the Anglican bishops in southern Africa had embraced the renewal and were encouraging the movement of the Holy Spirit in their dioceses. Although Archbishop Bill had only been in his new diocese for a comparatively short time, the clergy who were out of step were those not moving in the renewing power of the Spirit, rather than those who were.

During the second week of my visit evening seminars for clergy and lay leaders had been arranged. It was envisaged that about 150 people would gather for times of solid teaching. After the events in the cathedral during the previous week, it was impossible to keep people away. St. John's, Wynberg, is fairly large and was built originally as a garrison church. It was packed to overflowing each evening and again we saw the Spirit of God moving in powerful ways.

It was such a privilege to see the Lord working like this. Sometimes I would stand before the crowds of people and think to myself: "What am I doing here, so far from home? What right do I have to speak to all these people and know that the lives of many are going to be deeply affected as a result?" The Lord was the answer to such questions. He had brought me to this place. Only He could anoint anyone with authority to speak in His name. And if lives were going to be affected that would be through the activity of His Spirit.

Above all, it was good to see Bill's sensitive spiritual leadership. He chaired every one of the main mission meetings during that fortnight. Knowing how busy he was, it was a wonder that he could arrange to be present every night. However, it is a cardinal principle of spiritual leadership that you lead by example. Many of the clergy and a great host of people of that diocese were following the example set by their archbishop and were meeting with the Lord in the power of His Holy Spirit.

I had visited one of the coloured townships for a day of renewal towards the end of my time in Cape Town. On the day before my departure, the brethren there delivered a large basket of delicious fruit as a token of thanks. It was a very touching gesture. However I could hardly carry all this fruit around the rest of South Africa with me; so I willingly made a gift of it to the Burnetts. Knowing my partiality for it they accepted the rest of the fruit only on condition that I ate the large pineapple which was at the centre of the beautiful arrangement. My objections were not heeded and that evening I waded through more fresh pineapple than I have ever eaten either before or since. It was delicious.

From Cape Town I moved on to Port Elizabeth where Bruce Evans, another Spirit-filled man, was bishop. On the Sunday I went to preach in an Anglican church in a black township just outside the city. There had been rioting only weeks before, including the burning down of a school near the church building.

I received an extraordinarily gracious welcome. The service was conducted in the Xhosa (pronounced: Causa) language by the archdeacon who was rector of the parish. This was my first experience of speaking with an interpreter and I found it strange and frustrating at first. Intensive concentration was required and so the sermon was shorter than usual. Instead of an extended period of ministry, I led the people in a short time of response in which they answered personally the question Jesus asked the blind beggar, Bartimaeus: "What do you want me to do for you?"

When I had resumed my seat the archdeacon addressed the congregation in Xhosa. He then said the me: "Now you pray for the people." Apparently he had made some kind of altar call and immediately about 200 people responded. I suggested that he join me in the laying on of hands. "No, no, *you* pray for the people."

I was not accustomed to the African attitude towards time. The people did not mind how long it took to pray with all these folk; they went on worshipping the Lord in song. I didn't know the need of each person, so prayed as much in tongues as English and simply believed God would meet each person in their need.

At the end of the service, I was ushered from the vestry back into the church. To my surpirse nobody had departed; everyone was still seated. In front of the congregation a table and chairs had been placed. I was shown to one of these. There followed a series of addresses from leading members of the congregation, a mixture of welcome, greetings and thanks. I was overwhelmed by the gratitude and the warmth that was shown. It was lunchtime before all the proceedings were finished and nobody seemed to mind. What an object-lesson to many Western congregations. I heard later they were disappointed the sermon had been so short!

At Grahamstown, I spoke to an afternoon meeting of clergy, ordinands from the theological college, and lay leaders. So many people arrived for the evening meeting that it could not take place in the arranged venue, so everyone went along the street to the cathedral. I had only been speaking for a few minutes when one of the bells began to ring in a most unmelodic way, accompanied by much banging and thumping. This persisted throughout the talk. I don't know how anyone could maintain concentration to listen; I certainly found it difficult to do so while speaking.

It was later explained that as the cathedral was not due to be used that evening one of the bells was being rehung. The moral of this story is — never have a renewal meeting in a cathedral when they are doing this to the bells! The amazing thing is that despite the noises off, many people were blessed by the Lord that evening.

From Grahamstown to East London, where I stayed with a community at the Christian Caring Centre. This community was headed by Derek Crumpton, one of the leading figures of the renewal in South Africa. In East London there was a series of evening meetings and seminars for ministers. The hunger of some men was reflected by the fact that a small group of ministers flew south for the meetings from Durban, as I was not going to visit Natal on this trip.

I was also faced with the harsh realities of life for some of our black brothers. I met two African priests who told me that one of their colleagues had been murdered in the recent period of rioting. He had been pulled from his vehicle and beaten to death by black militants because he had been worshipping with whites, and was preaching peace and reconciliation among the races.

These two priests knew that their names were also on the assassination list. They recognised that this must in no way compromise their determination both to teach and live the gospel of love. Their quiet courage was a tremendous witness of faith for the future, faith in Jesus our Lord, Saviour and King.

On the Saturday morning I caught an early flight for Johannesburg. I was met at the airport and rushed to a large church hall where I was to speak at a day of renewal, scheduled to begin at ten-thirty a.m. We arrived a few minutes before eleven o'clock to the sound of praise. People were packed into the hall like sardines; it was a very hot day and gathered outside every open door and window was a further group of people.

I began speaking from Romans 6–8. We are dead in Christ; the old life has been crucified that we might be set free to live the new life He gives us. Baptism signifies that the old nature is dead and buried and need no longer control our lives and actions. In Jesus we are made sons of God, filled with the Holy Spirit. We are to set our minds, not on the past, on what we were, but on things above, on the things of the Spirit and see the fruit of the Spirit being produced in our lives through His work within us. We have been delivered from dead, legalistic and formal religion and have been made sons of God. Now nothing can separate us from His love in Christ Jesus.

The hunger of the people seemed to draw out the teaching from the Word. At the end of the day I had spoken in all for about five hours. It was not so much me teaching others, but the Holy Spirit teaching all of us. I find it exciting that He opens up the Word to our hearts in this way.

About three years later, I attended a leaders' conference in

Singapore at which one of the delegates was a coloured priest from Cape Town. He greeted me with a big hug.

"I have something wonderful I want to tell you," he said. "For many years my brother had been resisting the Lord. He lived such a worldly life that it seemed we had nothing in common. I decided I could have nothing more to do with him and told him that, as far as I was concerned, he was no longer my brother.

"He and my sister lived in Johannesburg. She was a Christian but found life very trying because of my brother's unbelief. She wanted to come to the day of renewal and persuaded my brother to drive her to the venue. When they arrived, she suggested that he might as well stay as he had nothing else to do. After some encouragement he agreed.

"My brother tried not to listen at first, but then he realised that God was telling him that his way of life needed to change. When it came to the time of ministry at the end of the day, he gave his life to the Lord.

"That evening he telephoned me in Cape Town. Amid the tears all he could say at first was: 'You have your brother back'." The dear brother was almost in tears himself as he recounted the story. Truly we have been given the gospel of reconciliation — of man to God, and brother to brother.

That is just one testimony. When the Spirit of God moves powerfully at a meeting, He alone knows the hundreds of works that He has accomplished in the hearts of His people.

After ministering for five hours in the heat I felt exhausted. That must have been obvious to others: "It's the altitude," they assessed. Johannesburg is over a mile above sea level. The high altitude means that the air is thinner and this causes tiredness until the blood has become accustomed to the change in atmosphere. But that was not the end of the day. I was then driven to Pretoria where I was to be staying with the bishop, Michael Nuttall, and his wife. They had arranged a barbeque as a welcome and had invited some of the leading figures in the diocese.

They took one look at me and thought I should go to bed.

I persuaded them that a short rest would suffice if they could excuse me for the early part of the proceedings. I lay down for half an hour and recovered sufficiently to face both food and people. Despite my protestations I was made to submit to examination by a doctor who was present. He thought I looked so shattered that something must be wrong with my heart. I assured him that all I needed was a good night's sleep and I would be ready to minister in the morning.

After the examination he was reassured. After a good night's sleep I was indeed raring to go. Now I had a better mental attitude towards fatigue.

I have found over the years that the Holy Spirit enables me to minister no matter what my physical condition. If I am feeling unwell beforehand I can't wait to begin speaking. As soon as I do so, I shall feel fine. Sometimes symptoms or tiredness may return afterwards, but God in His graciousness always enables the time of ministry in His name.

On the Sunday there was a day of renewal in the cathedral at Pretoria. Again the same hunger was evident. A group of nuns had travelled all the way from Salisbury, Rhodesia, to be present and on subsequent days of teaching, many clergy and leaders travelled hundreds of miles from remote parts of the diocese.

My last engagement on the tour of South Africa was to speak in a Dutch Reformed church, where Andreas Lombard was the dominie. When it was known that a renewed Anglican priest was to speak in a Dutch Reformed church, the news was greeted with incredulity by most people. Such a thing was unheard of. Although the official policy of that denomination was totally against renewal, about 150 of Andreas's people had been baptised in the Holy Spirit. That evening we experienced our unity in the Spirit as the Lord moved among us.

For Andreas the writing was already on the wall. A few days later he was due to appear before the leaders of the denomination. I later heard that he had been dismissed. Such can be the cost of obedience to the Lord. That released him to a wider ministry and he began an organisation to encourage renewal among the Afrikaans-speaking people. He also became pastor of a Presbyterian congregation in Pretoria which I visited on a subsequent tour of South Africa.

I returned to England excited by the spiritual climate of that country. What a beautiful place, and yet what a sad one! But I had seen the Holy Spirit moving with greater freedom than I had experienced elsewhere. The news we receive in Britain concentrates on the racial issues; it is not newsworthy material for the media that God is at work in a wonderful way despite the political situation.

6 Renewal of Faith

BACK TO BRITAIN and more meetings! My engagements were arranged about eighteeen months in advance and I had not planned sufficient time to recover from the tour to South Africa. I was at home for only a few days, catching up with correspondence and my family at the same time, before I was off again. Cheltenham, Worcester, Scotland, Derby, Elim Bible College, Sidcup, Aldershot, Farnborough, Leicester, York, Northampton, Twickenham, Stoke and Bradford.

Fortunately I had set aside a three-week period in May for writing and studying. It had not seemed right to accept any speaking engagements during that period; I needed time to be fed and renewed myself. In the event, the time had to be spent in a different way.

The remainder of the household had been battling with me to rest more. I had recognised the need to do so, but had not taken the necessary steps to make it possible. A doctor pointed out to a Christian patient: "Even the Lord God Almighty had one day off in seven!" There is no answer to that!

I had been away from home for eight of the first twelve weeks of that year. It was time that I gave more of myself to my wife and children. Instead of spending the time in study (for which I was too tired) it seemed that the Lord was saying I should take the family for a good holiday, when we could simply enjoy each other and I could be thoroughly rested.

It seemed right that we should head for the sun. However,

we are not very good at spending money on ourselves and have always been accustomed to inexpensive holidays. On investigation we were surprised to discover that it was relatively inexpensive to go to Spain out of season on a package deal. We still did not have the necessary money.

Day after day I laid the matter before the Lord; no money was forthcoming. I was sure it was not my desire to take the family abroad; I had travelled enough in the past year. If this was what the Lord was saying why did He not supply the necessary cash?

One day the children discovered the brochures I had been perusing. That started the questions, and the excitement. The idea of flying, of going abroad, of staying in a hotel. They could not believe it possible! "If you want to go, you will have to ask the Lord to supply the money," I told them.

That night Claire (our eldest) prayed and the following morning the necessary money arrived! She was overjoyed and we all rejoiced with her. I had to seek an explanation from the Lord; for days I had been praying without result! The answer was simple. The Lord pointed out to me that I had wanted to take my wife and children away. He wanted this holiday to be a gift to all of us from Him. Our heavenly Father was taking us all away on holiday. The children needed to see that this was a gift from their heavenly Father, not their earthly one!

Claire was greatly encouraged by the way her prayer was answered.

About this time George and Hazel Hoerder, a lovely Christian couple living near us in East Molesey, joined our team. George had recently retired from the army with the rank of brigadier and agreed to take over the administrative side of our ministry. For this I was profoundly thankful. It was never possible to keep up with the piles of correspondence, especially after a time abroad. George immediately brought some military efficiency to our affairs. Being a sensitive man spiritually, he could answer many queries on my behalf and only referred essential matters to me. Both he and Hazel were a great encouragement in fellowship and prayer and were a great help to Caroline when I was away from home.

George has another great asset; he loves cricket. Our occasional visits to Lord's have been a great treat over the years.

With George taking care of the administration a great burden had been lifted from me. The holiday in Spain did marvels physically, and it was great, on my return, to be able to minister without feeling completely drained of energy afterwards.

However, as the summer of 1977 wore on, I was becoming aware of another need, a spiritual one. While in Luton, there had been a constant progression in my spiritual life. I had to seek the Lord continually for his direction so that I could lead others in the ways of His Spirit. God was always facing us with new things, new challenges, taking us to new and deeper places with Himself.

I now realised how much I had missed being part of a body moving on with God. Although I had learned a great deal in the past eighteen months of travelling and had seen Him at work in wonderful ways, yet there was something missing. I was spiritually jaded.

What was lacking? The Lord showed me that I had faithfully sought Him for the ministry, but I had stopped seeking Him for Himself. I was no longer breaking through to new places with Him. He wanted to reveal Himself to me in new ways and deepen my understanding of Himself. There were many things that He could then teach me that would make my ministry to others far more fruitful.

A new repentance was needed — not simply saying "sorry" to the Lord, but a detailed re-offering and dedication of my life to Him. In July I was due to speak at Haldon Court, a Christian hotel in Exmouth. As it was a holiday week, the demands of ministry were not great. The rest of the time could be devoted to seeking the Lord.

I went carefully through each area of my life, asking the Holy Spirit to show me where repentance was needed. I had disobeyed the Lord in taking on too much ministry. Because of tiredness I had grown lax in spiritual discipline in some ways. I no longer arose for prayer as early as I used to. I had prayed about the ministry but had not interceded in other ways as I could have done. And so on. I wrote all these things down, and other things too: wrong attitudes towards others, neglect of giving to my family because I was so busy. All had to be brought to the cross.

I knelt and began to pour out all these things to the Lord. As I prayed there was a tremendous sense of the Lord's presence. His peace descended on me; I was completely forgiven. His joy filled my heart and I was bursting to sing God's praises in a way I had not experienced in a long time. I was filled with such gratitude towards Him for His faithfulness; once more He had demonstrated His love and mercy. He had shown again that true repentance always leads to a fresh release of the Holy Spirit's activity in our lives.

Needing to praise the Lord without disturbing others, I drove to an area of heathland where I walked for hours praising the Lord in tongues at the top of my voice. Whenever I had to pass near other people the volume would diminish until they were out of earshot.

As I walked along, enjoying this new release of praise in my heart, I felt that the Lord was telling me to look at the sky. Instead of the clouds moving in one direction they suddenly seemed to move in all four directions at once, outwards from a central point. As they did so, the rays of the sun penetrated. I stood watching, awestruck. What did this mean? I couldn't tell, but I sensed that God was about to do something important in my life.

Towards the end of September I returned to Australia; this time I would not arrive exhausted. I first went to Canberra, where I was to conduct a mission at O'Connor United Church. The Methodists had joined with Presbyterians and Congregationalists to form a new denomination since my previous visit nearly eighteen months before. This was the church where Harry Westcott was the minister.

Harry is a dynamic character. He had courageously led the whole church into renewal, despite stiff opposition at times. There was a keen concern for evangelism and the congregation had grown appreciably; the modern building could hardly contain the people any longer.

The church was at a crisis point. Anybody who has led a con-gregation forward in the things of God, knows that a number of crises have to be encountered along the way. At such times God faces His people with the need to move on in obedience to Him in the spiritual pilgrimage on which He is taking them. Any rebellion that may be in people's hearts becomes exposed.

O'Connor was facing one of the most crucial matters: our commitment to one another. I knew from my experience at St. Hugh's how difficult it was to face the new commandment of Jesus, to love one another as He has loved us. During my travels I discovered this was the sticking point for many congregations. If they are not prepared to face this issue the blessing and anoint-ing of God will diminish.

It is great to be blessed individually by the Lord, to receive His forgiveness, to know His acceptance and love, to be filled with His Spirit, to receive gifts and healings. But feelings of love are not enough. Love has to be put into action. If our love for God is genuine, our commitment to others will be apparent. "For anyone who does not love his brother, whom he has seen, cannot love God, whom he has not seen." (1 John 4:20). In the four days of that mission the Lord took most people apart and then put them together again, Harry included.

It was a time of repentance and therefore of blessing. The church could now move on in faithful obedience and did — as a subsequent visit was to prove.

From Canberra I went to Sydney, where my first engagement was to speak at a city-wide day of renewal in the ballroom of the Hilton Hotel. The other speaker was a black independent Pentecostal from America. What a mixture of reactions I had to his ministry! To me he seemed to take some Scriptures out of context and make them mean whatever he wanted. There was much emphasis on personal ambition and material prosperity; and when he led the time of personal ministry at the end of the day I was utterly perplexed.

Many hundreds indicated that they wished to receive the laying on of hands. They were ushered out of their places in lines along the entire length of the ballroom. The pastor walked along the line laying hands on some, touching the foreheads of others, sometimes only waving a hand over a person. And down nearly everyone went, falling backwards to be caught by those who walked behind the line, and laid to rest on the floor.

I had encountered this phenomenon before but had never seen an exhibition such as this. Was it genuine? Was this really the Holy Spirit at work? Some stayed on the floor for a short while but most rose to their feet again immediately. I could not see the purpose of it. The impression was given that to go down was an indication that you were open to receive the power and healing of God. "There's your healing. That's your healing. Receive your healing. Don't resist the Lord." Such were the things that were being said.

To me this seemed like spiritual gymnastics — an assessment I felt was confirmed when the pastor asked those who had already received healing to raise a hand. Very few hands were raised despite the fact that hundreds had received "ministry"!

And yet I saw in this man a quality of faith that I had never seen in anyone else. And that was real: it was genuine. He believed implicitly in the promises of Scripture. If God said He will do it, He will do it. He taught that to believe contrary circumstances was to disbelieve God in that situation. I found his style of teaching and ministering difficult, but I knew that I needed the quality of faith that he possessed.

When you see something in another's life or ministry that you want or need, it is possible to react in a number of ways. Some feel jealous towards the person concerned, and are resentful towards God because He has not given them that same quality or gift. Others feel inferior. They have a negative and defeated attitude. "That's all right for him, but God would not want to do such a thing in my life." Alternatively, a person can say to God: "That is what I need in my life. Lord, show me how I can receive that quality." That was my prayer. "Lord, I don't want that man's style of ministry, but I do want that kind of faith."

The disquiet in my own soul during the summer, and the subsequent seeking of the Lord to break through to a new place with Him, were part of a greater disquiet. For some time I had been concerned about the state of the renewal in Britain. In the early seventies there had been considerable emphasis upon experience and the miraculous power of the Holy Spirit. The past three or four years had been a period of consolidation. Solid teaching was necessary so that people were not simply going from one experience to another.

During these latter years a great number of people had come into blessing and had been baptised in the Holy Spirit. They had become part of what was increasingly known as "the renewal". But coming into the movement at a time when the current emphasis was on solid teaching, many had never known first-hand experience of the miracles, the happenings, the events of former years.

There were many churches and prayer groups that had once known these happenings taking place regularly, but which had now almost lost sight of the miraculous. It could hardly be true to say that they had grown beyond such things; miracles were present throughout the ministry of Jesus. There had been a diminishing of faith in God to act in powerful ways, although those dimensions of the Spirit's activity were not lost completely and miracles had not ceased to happen. God wanted us to add teaching to the power; not replace the one with the other.

Was there a general lack of faith? Was that the heart of the problem? For Jesus, prayer and faith went together. You could not imagine Him praying without faith that His Father would answer Him. How many prayers did I pray without that same expectation? Too many! I needed that added dimension of faith that now I saw was possible. I turned to the words of Scripture and read again and again the prayer promises of Jesus. As I did so the Holy Spirit began to speak them to my heart.

I will do whatever you ask in my name, so that the Son may bring glory to the Father. (John 14:13)
You may ask me for anything in my name, and I will do it. (John 14:14)

If you remain in me and my words remain in you, ask whatever you wish, and it will be given you. (John 15:7)

You did not choose me, but I chose you to go and bear fruit, fruit that will last. Then the Father will give you whatever you ask in my name. (John 15:16)

I tell you the truth, my Father will give you whatever you ask in my name. (John 16:23)

Ask and you will receive, and your joy will be complete. (John 16:24)

I tell you the truth, if you have faith as small as a mustard seed, you can say to this mountain, "Move from here to there" and it will move. Nothing will be impossible for you. (Matt. 17:20)

Again, I tell you that if two of you on earth agree about anything you ask for, it will be done for you by my Father in heaven. (Matt. 18:19)

Therefore, I tell you, whatever you ask for in prayer, believe that you have received it, and it will be yours. (Mark 11:24)

So I say to you: "Ask and it will be given to you ..." for everyone who asks receives. (Luke 11:9, 10)

Either Jesus meant what He said, or He didnt. If He is the truth He is not going to deceive His people by giving them false promises. To suggest that these are not authentic words of Jesus is simply an excuse for unbelief.

As we grow in the Lord there is to be an increase, not a diminishing of faith. Faith, as Jesus taught it, resulted in God intervening in the daily circumstances and needs of people's lives. Faith for Him had dynamic consequences and was directly linked with prayer: "You may ask me for anything ..."; "ask whatever you wish ..."; "whatever you ask ..."; "ask"; "if you have faith ...".

And the promises He gives: "I will do it." "It will be given you." "The Father will give you whatever you ask in my name." "You will receive." "Nothing will be impossible for you." "It will be done for you by my Father in heaven." "Believe that you have received it, and it will be yours." "For everyone who asks receives."

Faith comes from hearing the Word of God spoken to your heart by the Holy Spirit. Words that before were merely words now leap to life in a new way. That is what I was experiencing as I continued to minister in Sydney. Of course Jesus meant what He said; of course God would answer if we came to Him in faith. Or would He? Very quickly this new-found confidence was put to the test.

Once again, I was suffering from excruciating pain. Late that evening I asked the young couple with whom I was staying to minister to me and together we prayed the prayer of faith: "Whatever you ask for in prayer, believe that you have received it, and it will be yours." I was to heed the words of Jesus, not the circumstances. I was to believe I had received the healing I needed.

I went upstairs to bed thanking the Lord for His answer and trying to ignore the pain, which had eased but was still present. It had been a long day and when I flopped into bed, I soon fell asleep with sheer fatigue. But not for long.

I awoke with the pain worse than ever. "Believe that you have received it. Believe that you have received it. Believe that you have received it." Over and over again those words ran through my mind. I prayed and prayed, thanking the Lord for His healing, rebuking the symptoms in the name of Jesus and telling the enemy that he was already defeated in the situation.

Meanwhile the pain was so bad I was alternately pacing the floor and throwing myself on the bed, trying to find the position of least discomfort. For two hours this persisted. This was a battle of faith, a battle that had to be won; I must persevere. Home seemed every bit of 12,000 miles away!

After two hours or more, the Lord spoke quietly to me: "Go to bed and go to sleep." That had to be Him speaking if this was going to be possible. There was no other way that I could fall asleep in such pain. I got back into bed and within a few minutes was sound asleep. When I awoke, I felt refreshed and the pain had disappeared, apart from a slight sensation that persisted for about a week, as the Lord taught me how to hold on in faith and not doubt the healing.

A new dimension of faith was present in my attitude towards everything, and this affected my preaching and ministry. There was a new confidence and expectancy that God would meet with people in His power. I was used to Him working quietly in their lives; now I sensed there would be clear demonstrations of His miraculous interventions.

And then the worst possible thing happened. I was praying for a number of folk to be healed at the end of a meeting as they knelt in good order at the communion rail. While I was laying hands on one man, suddenly he was gone. He had keeled over backwards and lay on the floor, seemingly oblivious to everything. "No, Lord, no! Not that! I want the faith; but not that." I held on to others so that they couldn't fall as I prayed for them. My mind was in turmoil.

After the service the man concerned came to see me. "That was marvellous," he said. "I've never experienced anything like it before; such a sense of the Lord's peace. I feel completely different."

I nodded, trying to make it appear that nothing untoward had happened. At least the man hadn't immediatly sprung up, but had laid on the floor for some time; the Lord must have ministered to him in some way.

In Brisbane I led a weekend on "Renewal of Faith". As I spoke about the prayer promises of Jesus my own faith, as well as that of others, was being enlarged.

In Melbourne, there were two evening services in the cathedral. At the second of these, a spirit of praise came upon the congregation and that great building echoed to the joyful praises of God's people and the harmonies of singing in the Spirit. Many suggested that in its history that was the first time that the cathedral had known such worship. "The building will never be the same again," they commented with supreme optimism.

At least in Melbourne the crowds of people were too great to allow for any personal laying on of hands. So I was saved from the dilemma caused by people falling down! Not so at my next venue in Tasmania.

In prayer before the service, I laid this matter before God. "Lord, I do not want to resist your purposes in any way; neither do I want to become involved in anything that is dishonouring to your name. I ask you not to allow anyone to fall down if this is not your purpose. But I submit my will to yours. If this is your purpose, please give me some undeniable evidence of the fact tonight."

Towards the end of the meeting a number of people came forward for healing. All except for one man, fell to the floor when I prayed for them and he was so unsteady a chair had to be brought for him.

"All right, Lord; you win!"

On the following Saturday evening, about 900 were packed into a church in the centre of Adelaide. While praying with some clergy and leaders before the meeting, I was thankful there would be so many to help in the time of ministry. "Only you are to lay hands on people tonight." Although I recognised the voice, I tried to push the words away. Why should the Lord say such a thing? Once I began to speak, the idea was quickly forgotten.

At the end of the talk, I invited people to come forward for prayer if they were seeking the Lord in some specific way. I was totally unprepared for the response. Immediately 500 people, or more, got to their feet and came surging forward like a tidal wave. My immediate reaction was to look round for help from other clergy. I could not catch anybody's eye; each was as staggered as I at the response. And then I heard the Lord again, "Only you are to lay hands on these people."

I could only pray briefly with each: "Receive your healing in the name of Jesus and for His glory" — or similar words. Soon I started laying hands on two people at the same time. Some fell immediately to the ground; others did not. It didn't trouble me either way; I had given the whole matter to the Lord. Some soon got to their feet; others were on the ground for a prolonged time. When people saw the power of God at work, they too came forward for prayer. I knew that He was doing mighty things.

And there were humorous touches too. Some were determined they were not going to fall to the ground, but down they went! Two women had their arms interlinked and were holding on to one another for dear life. I prayed for them together and down they went, their arms intertwined.

After the service I apologised to the other ministers for not asking them to help with the time of ministry. To my surprise, they said that normally they would have come forward as a matter of course, but each had felt the Holy Spirit restraining them and telling them not to do so. Still I could not understand why.

My last engagement in Australia was to be at Salisbury United Church, a few miles out of Adelaide. I mentioned my dilemma to the minister there about being the only one to administer the laying on of hands on Saturday evening. The Lord had given him a simple explanation. He had not wanted people to start making invidious comparisons between what happened when different ministers prayed. It was so apparent that the power of God was at work that everybody had their eyes on Him, where they needed to be. "That is the wisdom of the Lord," he said; "so different from the wisdom of men." He was right. I had been deeply worried that it might have appeared that I wanted to draw attention to myself, or monopolise the ministry; and all the time, the Lord was ensuring that the attention of the people should not be directed to me personally.

The church building was packed with people for the meeting. News of what had happened on Saturday night had spread and there was a great sense of expectancy. The interest of a number of unconverted people had been aroused. As I was preparing to speak, there was great certainty in my heart that God was going to work in really powerful ways. I knew it. Yet the Word He gave me to speak was not about faith or power, but about being a people of praise.

When folk began to come forward for ministry the power of the Lord came upon them. That encouraged others to come. One could see a repercussive effect running through the congregation. Unconverted men came forward, kneeling with tears in their eyes and asking God for mercy. Even young children were falling on their knees and meeting with the Saviour. The power of God was coming upon many long before I, or anyone else, could get near them to pray.

I had never seen such an astonishing sight. It was impossible to question the reality of what was happening. No doubt there will be those who will want to dismiss this as emotionalism or to give some psychological explanation. You had to be present to know that there was only one true reason for what was happening: God was at work among His people.

One lady was still prostrate long after the end of the service. "What has the Lord been doing?" I asked her when she returned to consciousness.

"Showing me who is boss," was her simple reply.

Her pastor told me she was a woman who had been a great concern to him. She had received much ministry but had stubbornly refused to submit to the Lord's authority in her life. This had prevented her receiving the healing that she had needed. During the hour or so that she was on the floor, this woman experienced a real encounter with the Lord, who spoke directly to the cause of her rebellion. I could now see at least one good reason for this strange phenomenon.

Before returning to England, I flew to Auckland, New Zealand. There I was to lead a weekend of renewal in St. Paul's Church, a centre of renewal for some years and particularly known for its music ministry. The theme of the weekend was again a "Renewal of Faith".

I knew I had to be careful not to major on this subject unless it was the Word of God in the particular situation where I was to minister. During several conversations with members of the community at St. Paul's, it became obvious that a renewal of faith was precisely what was required. This visit was another example of the Lord's planning and timing. St. Paul's had experienced what I had noticed in Britain. Once the power of the Spirit, and the happenings of God, had been more apparent than they were now. But as the Holy Spirit ministered the prayer promises of Jesus to people's hearts, faith was encouraged again.

In subsequent months I sought to understand this phenomenon of falling under the power of the Spirit and questioned many people closely about what happened to them. Three categories seem to emerge:

1. There are those who fall and almost immediately return to their former position, either standing or kneeling. Their falling to the ground appears to signify little. Some may believe it is expected of them, or that they have to do so to receive God's blessing or healing. It could be subconsciously self-induced, therefore, even if there is no deliberate intention to fall down for the sake of it.

However, this cannot account for all in this category. Many have told me that at the moment the band has touched their head the power of God has shot through their whole body like an electric shock that literally knocks them off balance. They had no desire or intention to fall, but were unable to remain on their feet.

2. There are those who fall to the ground and stay there for a short time, usually between five and ten minutes. They are not unconscious, being aware of what is going on around them and able to hear when spoken to. However, they experience a tremendous sense of the presence of God, especially of His peace. They feel so peaceful they desire neither to move nor to communicate with others.

Such an experience brings considerable healing to people and God deals with areas of anxiety that have contributed to emotional or physical sickness.

3. There are those who fall completely unconscious for a longer time, usually about twenty minutes, although it can be for much longer periods, as with the lady mentioned above. During this time, the Lord deals in truly significant ways with

them, often producing inner healing as the Spirit reaches deep within the person's being, deeper than any ministry at a conscious level could produce.

Some, to whom I have spoken, testify to truly remarkable experiences of the Lord. A few, perhaps, have a small foretaste of heaven. No observer could be certain of that.

So although this phenomenon could sometimes be psychologically induced, I saw enough to convince me of the genuine work that God was doing in many. It used to distress me to hear some Christians dismiss this almost with derision, without first-hand experience of it, or attempting to understand what was happening to people.

However, I was determined never to encourage this phenomenon. The emphasis needed to be on the Lord Himself and our coming to Him with faith, not on some manifestation of the effects of His power upon people. It was possible to receive healing whether standing, kneeling, sitting or prostrate.

At the end of each trip Caroline would brace herself for my return, for on each occasion, she received home a different husband! That had been the story of our marriage: Caroline had to adjust to the constant changes that were taking place in me. From my Australian letters she knew she was in for yet another adjustment.

On the flight home I had time to reflect on the events of the past few weeks. So much had happened and yet there was one thing of unsurpassed importance: I had never known a time when I had been closer to the Lord. He was truly at the centre of everything and it was no hardship for my thoughts to be centred on Him. When I prayed I knew that He was going to answer and give me what I asked. It seemed that all ungodly desires had passed away; I no longer had to fight them. Jesus in all His love and holiness and power was everything to me. I wish life had been like that ever since; sadly that is not the case.

On the way home the Lord demonstrated His love and willingness to answer prayer in a trivial incident and yet one that remains vivid in my memory. Singapore Airlines are renowned for their service and frequently produce fruit juice to refresh you, both with and between meals. On my particular flight they were majoring on pineapple juice. Now I like pineapple juice in moderation. But it tends to be sweet and I do not have a very sweet tooth.

Again it was time for a meal, and again it was pineapple juice. I could see it clearly as the trays were being distributed. I definitely could not take any more. "Ask whatever you wish . . ." Those words had become very significant in recent weeks, but in far more important circumstances. However, the Lord said "Whatever", and He meant what He said.

"Lord, I really would prefer orange juice. I don't know how you are going to provide that because I can see all the trays have pineapple juice. But I believe you can do it. Thank you."

Within seconds, a stewardess served me with a tray from behind and there was a container of orange juice. Everybody else in that cabin was served from the front with pineapple — and there was the orange juice in front of me. I sat there thankful, not so much for the orange juice as for the Father's love and faithfulness in keeping His Word, even in such a trivial way. I was aware of His care and concern even for small details.

There have been many occasions since when I have needed to see the Lord act in important ways, and have been reminded of this incident. If God can answer trivial desires, is He not ready to meet with us in more significant needs?

7   Trust Me

CAROLINE SOON discovered how very different her husband was, far more positive in his attitude towards everything. Negative statements and attitudes jarred; they were a denial of faith. We needed to be positive in our approach to every situation and that was a particular challenge to her.

It was such a blessing to know the presence of the Lord so intimately that I was full of praise and love for Him, much more than ever before. That can be very frustrating for those around you. I tried to "play it cool", but it was not easy.

Although it had been a physically demanding tour I was anxious to start ministering in Britain. I knew this message of faith was so desperately needed here. The Spirit of God moved powerfully each evening of a teaching mission I was leading in Tunbridge Wells and many experienced a renewal of faith. On the Saturday I was so aware of the power of God it was difficult to stay on my feet both while preaching and ministering afterwards. That is as close as I have ever been to falling under the power of the Spirit myself.

The Lord did some mighty things in those days as He also did during the following week in Cornwall, where I was the guest of evangelist Don Double for the Cornwall Renewal meetings. Normally, the Cornish folk are reticent to come forward for personal ministry, I was told, but there was no evidence of that on this occasion. The Lord was speaking clearly to people and encouraging faith to believe Him to meet with them in their needs.

Don's faith was encouraged by the words of Jesus: "Ask whatever you wish . . .". He was in need of a new car for his extensive travelling ministry. He is a large man, not only in faith, but also in height and breadth. He needed a fairly large car to accommodate him comfortably, so he prayed: "Lord, you know I need a new car — and I would like it to be a Rover." He could not afford one, but if the Lord said he could have the car he wanted . . . Within a matter of days Don took delivery of a new Rover, despite the fact that there was a waiting list of several months for that particular model; someone "just happened" to cancel an order. He referred to it as his faith car.

Of greater significance was the healing of Joanna Sibthorpe, an eleven-year-old whose eyes had been filled with molten lead while Caroline and I were staying with her family in Truro. The teaching had to be worked out in experience!

In Manchester the teaching on faith met a need in just about everybody. All have a need to pray and many feel frustrated failures because of the lack of power and fruitfulness in their praying. The conference situation gave more time to develop teaching from the Word, and to see the Lord building faith and expectancy in the hearts of people to see mountains of need removed. Many were drawn to repentance for previous failure to trust God or to persevere with faith about a particular need, and received His assurance of forgiveness together with a gift of faith for the future.

By the final session on the Sunday afternoon, many people were meeting with God in powerful ways. What a contrast I was to experience on the following day. We crossed the Pennines to Leeds, full of joy and anticipation because of all that we had seen the Lord do recently. Here the atmosphere seemed spiritually cold by comparison. The church building was full and I asked people to raise a hand if they believed God was going to do mighty things in the lives of His people that night. Very few hands were raised.

What a confirmation to the things I had sensed about the general state of faith in the renewal. Many people do not expect God to move in power when they go to church services on

Sundays. It is all too common to hear of people threatening to leave congregations if God is actually allowed to do anything powerful! When people come to a renewal gathering without expectation that God will be doing important things among His people, something is seriously wrong. St. Paul reminds us that "the kingdom of God is not a matter of talk but of power." (1 Cor. 4:20) To the Thessalonians he wrote: "Our gospel came to you not simply with words, but also with power, with the Holy Spirit and with deep conviction." (1 Thess. 1:5) And to the Romans he said: "I will not venture to speak of anything except what Christ has accomplished through me in leading the Gentiles to obey God by what I have said and done — by the power of signs and miracles, through the power of the Spirit." (Rom. 15:18–19)

Paul expected to communicate the gospel of God's Kingdom through the signs and miracles of God's power, as well as through words. In this he was following the example of Jesus and obeying the commission that He gave to His disciples: "As you go, preach this message: 'The kingdom of heaven is near.' Heal the sick, raise the dead, cleanse those who have leprosy, drive out demons. Freely you have received, freely give." (Matt. 10:7–8)

To try to explain away the miraculous and supernatural elements of the gospel is clearly lack of faith. Similarly, to say that the signs and wonders were for the apostolic age and not for today, is not only factually untrue; such an attitude denies faith in the Word of God and the promises of Jesus.

The low level of faith in Britain is a reflection of the low level of faith in the churches generally. And faith was not going to be re-established in the churches unless those who claimed to be filled with the Holy Spirit demonstrated a faith-full witness that clearly expected God to intervene in the affairs of men.

Often when Jesus spoke He caused division among His hearers because of their varying responses to what He said: a division between those who would obey and the disobedient, between those who believed and those who did not. "Whoever believes in him is not condemned, but whoever does not believe stands condemned already because he has not believed in the name of God's one and only Son." (John 3:18) "I tell you the truth, whoever hears my word and believes him who sent me has eternal life and will not be condemned; he has crossed over from death to life." (John 5:24)

Jesus spoke clearly of the rewards of faith, and warned equally clearly of the consequences of unbelief. And faith in the New Testament is not confined to some initial act of trust that is placed in Jesus Christ. Paul asked the Galatians those pertinent questions: "Did you receive the Spirit by observing the law, or by believing what you heard? Are you so foolish? After beginning with the Spirit, are you now trying to attain your goal by human effort? ... Does God give you his Spirit and work miracles among you because you observe the law, or because you believe what you heard?" (Gal. 3:2–3, 5)

After the initial act of faith there is the temptation to return to trying to please God by legalistic religious observance. There is also the tendency to replace dependence on the resources of His Spirit with self-effort and striving. Paul regards such action as foolish, and even suggests that the Galatians must have been bewitched to have deserted the principle that led them to experience the power of the Holy Spirit in their lives and God working miraculously in their midst.

The principle by which you are to live, he is saying, is "believing what you heard", having faith in the Word of God and the promises of Jesus.

Striving and self-effort is sin, whether expressed personally or corporately. God teaches us to live by faith in the resources that He has made available to us, "every spiritual blessing in the heavenly places". These resources are released into our lives when we pray with faith. This is the way that God has chosen to work. He has accomplished everything in Jesus that would enable us to have life "in all its fullness". He gives us the prayer promises to indicate the way in which He wants to give to His children. It delights Him to see faith in their hearts, believing Him to release His power, His blessing and resources into their lives.

Some object that to believe the promises of Jesus is to be

simplistic. I wonder if they would dare to make the same charges to Him face to face.

As I continued to teach on the scriptural principles of faith, I saw how closely the promises of God are linked to the fact that He has established a covenant relationship with His children, a new covenant sealed with the blood of Jesus. A covenant is a binding agreement between two parties. God did not have to bind Himself to men in such a way; He chose to do so. Having entered into such an agreement, He has bound Himself to keep His Word. It is for us to believe what He says and see the promises of God fulfilled in our lives.

The Holy Spirit has an indispensable part to play in receiving faith, which is a gift of the Spirit and comes through the Spirit declaring the truth of God's Word to our hearts. He can enable the Christian to believe in situations where previously faith had seemed impossible.

God promises to meet with those who seek Him with their hearts. "All who seek find." Clearly there is a need to be honest with God. There is little point in putting on a veneer of faith to impress other people. The sin of unbelief can be cleansed away only by His forgiveness.

The conviction that this teaching on faith needed to be written in book form had grown stronger. There was never enough time with the spoken word to cover more than a small fraction of what it means to pray with faith. It would be useful to give a fuller exposition of the relevant Scriptures in a form that people could refer to easily in times of doubt or need. Looking back in my programme it is difficult to see how there was the time to write *Anything You Ask* during the early months of 1978. Somehow between engagements, it was finished. The writing flowed easily, and I was deeply aware of the anointing of the Holy Spirit throughout the task.

Praise God for the way in which He has used that book! A continuous flow of testimonies both verbal and written have been received, telling how the Lord has increased people's faith and transformed the effectiveness of their prayers. Many share about specific answers and healings they have received.

The illustration of rocket and tortoise answers to prayer seems to have been of particular help. When teaching the disciples to pray with faith, Jesus told them to "believe that you have received it", to see the answer already accomplished with the eyes of faith. And He gave the promise, "it will be yours". But He does not say that it will be yours *immediately*.

In experience, some prayers of faith do release an immediate answer, like rockets that are launched in heaven and arrive at their destination with great accuracy and at high speed. These are the kind of answers we all like to receive.

More persistent faith is required if the evidence of God's answer is not visible immediately; the answer moves slowly towards us more like a tortoise than a rocket. The test of faith is to persevere in prayer, as Jesus teaches, until the tortoise arrives. Unfortunately, it is all too easy to give up before then, an indication of the shakiness of the original act of faith.

From January until the end of April I ministered at no less than thirty-three centres in England. They were exciting months because of the response of people to the message of faith, and the grace and power of God that were manifestly at work.

However, 1978 was going to be an exciting year for other reasons as well. The whole of our ministry needed to expand as we were having to turn down a great number of invitations. It was impossible to respond to the host of invitations from individual congregations for a weekend of renewal, teaching and ministry. It seemed right that I should concentrate personally on the larger meetings and the opportunities to minister to clergy and leaders. The last two years had seen the new travelling ministry established; now the time was right to see the expansion of the team. We prayed that God would give us the right people.

The names that came immediately to mind were those of David and Jane Brown. They were part of the church family at St. Hugh's and had come to know Jesus only a few days before their wedding in 1972. All who wanted to be married there were asked to attend a preparation course at which they were told the good news of Jesus Christ. Those who responded to the gospel were led through repentance to new life in Him and were baptised in the Holy Spirit.

David and Jane were one of the couples who responded. On the evening when they gave their lives to the Lord, I prayed in the church with Jane while David was left sitting in my study. She laid her life before the Lord, asked Him to forgive her sin, her fear and doubt. She gave herself and her future to Him and we prayed for her to be filled with the Holy Spirit. God met with her immediately and her face shone with the radiancy of Jesus.

We returned to the study; it was David's turn. He took one look at Jane, jumped to his feet and said: "Right, let's go." He almost ran into the church in his eagerness. One look at Jane was enough to convince him. If it had happened to her, then it had to happen to him — and quickly! A few minutes later, David was also praising the Lord; he was a new creation in Christ Jesus, filled with the Holy Spirit.

Their devotion to Jesus never wavered from that beginning. By the time I left Luton nearly four years later, David was the parish treasurer and was in the leadership group. After my departure, he emerged as one to whom others increasingly looked for direction and help.

While staying with them for a weekend (I was preaching at St. Hugh's on the Sunday morning) in December, David and I went for a walk round the cold dark streets of Dunstable. Gently I outlined what I believed God was saying; that they should come and join the ministry team. It may seem that David was a strange choice. He had no formal theological training, but he loved the Lord deeply and was an extremely "nice guy". One sensed his tremendous potential. I was far from sure how he would receive the suggestion, though. Only a few months before he had moved to this bigger house in Dunstable, so that he could have a larger community household.

I need not have worried; the Lord had been preparing the way. He was staggered, not because the suggestion was outrageous, but because the Lord had been impressing upon him for some weeks that his life was to be linked with ours in some way. He had not shared this with Jane, fearful of her reaction after the upheaval of moving house, for she had plenty on her hands with young Joanna and another baby on the way. When David later shared my suggestion with her, he was staggered once again. The Lord had been saying the same thing to her and she had not dared to discuss it with David, for the same reasons!

At that time, we were not particularly close friends of the Browns and rarely saw them. It seemed a good idea that David should come on a ministry tour of the north-east with me. We would have the opportunity to wait upon the Lord together and David could see what was happening through the ministry, which had certainly developed in many ways since my time at St. Hugh's. He is very sensitive spiritually, learns quickly and is a man of prayer; soon we were at one in faith.

Jesus said: "Again, I tell you that if two of you on earth agree about anything you ask for, it will be done for you by my Father in heaven." (Matt. 18:19) In David, the Lord was supplying someone with whom I could agree in prayer, one who would believe with me. That would be a tremendous encouragement and the promise of God was there before us. If we were at one in the Spirit in our praying, then "it will be done for you by my Father in heaven."

We asked the Lord to provide a house large enough for our two families, plus the two or three single people who would be part of the team. This had to be a prayer of faith. The sale of the Browns's house would only realise about £8,000 once the mortgage had been paid, and we had no capital at all. The Lord had been faithful to His promise and had provided us with our daily needs, but we had nothing "stored up in barns". He had promised to provide whatever was necessary for this ministry, and now a larger house was necessary.

We needed to be specific when praying. Vague prayers receive vague answers; specific prayers receive specific answers. It would be convenient to move by the end of August, so that the children could settle into new schools. That month was the only respite in the year's travelling schedule when I would be available for the physical mechanics of the move. We felt confident before the Lord that He would supply our need by that time.

It is dangerous to give God time limits within which He must answer. In this case, we felt that God was assuring us that He would provide within that period. The Browns put their house on the market, and we thanked the Fountain Trust for the provision of their house and said that we would move by the end of August. That fitted in well with their plans; their team was also being enlarged and they were expecting Michael Barling to join them in September.

We were prepared to go anywhere that the Lord wanted to place us; but every time we contemplated touring estate agents looking for a suitable property, we lost our peace. A particular Scripture was laid on our hearts:

Trust in the Lord and do good;
    dwell in the land and enjoy safe pasture.
Delight yourself in the Lord
    and He will give you the desires of your heart.
Commit your way to the Lord;
    Trust in him and he will do this. (Ps. 37:3-5)

We were not to seek our own answer. God was our Father, who would provide a home for His children; the children do not have to seek a home for their Father. If we trusted Him we would see Him provide.

He was asking the most difficult thing of us: to do nothing except wait, trust Him and pray. Instinctively, we wanted to rush out to look for a house; instead all those fleshly reactions had to be rejected.

Weeks passed and nothing happened. Within me was a quiet assurance that God had the whole matter in hand and there was no need for concern. To look at the circumstances would create anxiety; we needed to keep our eyes on the Lord. He would put the right place before us at the right time.

Nicholas Rivett-Carnac had inherited, with other members of his family, a large country house in Suffolk. It was due to be sold at a very reasonable price. It was vast and needed a considerable amount of work to make it suitable. Nevertheless, we had not sought this place, it had been offered to us. Could this be God's provision?

We had no great convictions about this particular house and yet, strangely, felt that we must pursue the matter further. Our waiting on the Lord began in January and it was now April. This was the only place that had been suggested in that time and August was getting closer every day.

The house was to be auctioned in May. It was decided that Caroline would go to the sale with David and Jane; I would be thousands of miles away in Canada at that time. If this was the right house, it would be delivered into our hands somehow.

As the day of the sale approached, still no money arrived with which to bid for the house. Was it worth going to the sale? Yes, for it seemed that the Lord was testing everybody's faith, to see if we would trust Him right up to the last minute. Caroline, David and Jane duly went to the auction, still believing that, if it was right, it would become ours. They sat there listening to the bids and the house was sold for a ridiculously low sum, but not to us. There was no conviction that they should bid without money. So was it all a waste of time?

Not at all. We had come through a test to build faith in us, not destroy it; the Lord immediately released to us a gift of £5,000 for the work of the ministry. That would have been sufficient to form a deposit and would have made it possible to bid at the auction to secure the property. In His wisdom He had given the money after the sale, not before it. This obviously was not the place. Perhaps He was saying something else to us through these events.

Several weeks passed before we heard of a large manor house in Lincolnshire, owned by a Christian who wanted to use it for the Lord's work. It was even bigger than the previous house, set in the most beautiful surroundings but needing a great deal of structural work before it would be ready for occupation, and we did not have a great deal of time.

The Lord wanted to supply the best for His work; we needed

what was right to facilitate the ministry. Certainly, this house in Lincolnshire was the best imaginable as far as its setting was concerned. We had never seen any house in more beautiful surroundings. So again, the Lord brought all of us to a place of saying that we would be prepared to go there if that was the place that He had chosen despite the many inconveniences we would have to suffer if we were to do so. That was exceedingly important, for He was making sure that all of us were totally submitted to Him. We said we were prepared to go anywhere and it needed to be demonstrated that we meant what we said. The thought of trying to make a home in such an enormous house was daunting.

It was now mid-June; August was ominously close. Although for most of the time I was at peace about the situation, there were odd moments when I would go roaming around the house thinking: "You're mad, Colin. You have a responsibility to your family, the household, to David and Jane." Their house was now sold and they would have to move at the beginning of September.

Such thoughts were only doubts sown by the enemy. I would get them out of my system by speaking them to Caroline. Immediately I had to repent before the Lord. I was not to doubt Him for a moment. He said He would provide and provide He would.

By now it was clear to us that we needed to trust Him for a much bigger house than was originally intended. "You are thinking only of the next stage of the ministry," He showed us; "I know your needs beyond that. I am thinking several stages ahead. You will not want to keep moving every few months as the ministry continues to expand."

That made sense. Our whole vision had to be enlarged. I had only been concerned that I should have someone to assist me, and one or two others able to accept invitations I had to refuse. The Lord had something else in mind. We needed to seek Him with even more determination and receive a further vision of His purpose for us.

For one of those inexplicable reasons, when planning the

diary over a year before, I had felt it right to keep a three-week period clear of engagements. I could not explain why; it was simply not right before the Lord to do any speaking during that time.

These three weeks could now be used as a time of prayer and fasting, eating only an evening meal with the children. Usually at the beginning of such a time, the Lord turns His spotlight on your own heart, and we all went through a time of repentance. It may seem that such personal issues had nothing to do with the need of a house. But we were seeking the Lord for Himself — not a house!

I spent very little time praying for accommodation. The Lord had promised to provide that. I wanted to ensure that there was no hindrance in my life to our receiving His provision. When I did pray about the house, all I could hear the Lord saying was: "Trust me". Over and over again those were the two words that the still small voice spoke to my heart.

Throughout the three weeks I was aware of an incredible sense of God's peace. He showed me that in the years ahead the ministry was to grow and expand far beyond anything that I imagined or had vision for at that time. This would be His work, not mine. He would build according to His plan, not as the result of any man-invented scheme.

"Trust me"; and we were now into the beginning of July, only a few weeks from the deadline. If we were to buy a property it was almost too late. The Lord had not released any further funds sufficient to buy a house. Perhaps He was going to supply in some other way.

At the very end of those three weeks of prayer, I received what I had been waiting for — a clear word from God. I had said in Him: "Lord, if you are going to supply a place as big as you are suggesting, it will take a fortune to furnish it."

As clear as anything came His immediate reply: "When you leave this place you will need to take nothing with you."

I was so excited. After weeks and months of hearing only "Trust me" here was something that was specific and definite. I went rushing into the kitchen. "Darling, have you ever thought how we are going to furnish this large house that the Lord is going to supply?" I asked Caroline.

"Well, I have been wondering about that. I suppose if the Lord can supply the house, He can supply furniture as well — somehow."

"He has just told me that when we leave here we will need to take nothing with us."

On the following day, I had to go to the University of Kent, at Canterbury, the venue of the 1978 Lambeth Conference, when all the diocesan bishops of the worldwide Anglican Communion gather. It had been decided to hold an international conference of Anglican leaders involved in the renewal, prior to the Lambeth Conference. Many of the fifty Anglican bishops who publicly acknowledged their baptism in the Holy Spirit would be in Britain and this seemed too good an opportunity to miss.

Being one of the organising committee I went to Canterbury for the weekend before the conference. A core group of about twenty were to spend the weekend in prayer seeking the Lord's guidance. This was a spiritually "high-powered" group including many I knew to be men of prayer, sensitive to the voice of the Spirit.

No matter how sure we are of hearing the Lord's voice, we should never be afraid of submitting what we have heard to others. To fail to do this is an evidence of insecurity, not assurance. So I asked a small group of seven or eight to pray with me. Guess what they heard? "Trust me!" That was the essence of the prophetic visions and words received. There was confidence that the Lord was promising to provide and was about to do so.

One of the pictures that the Lord gave was of a ship that had been tied up at its berth. All the mooring lines had been released except one, and this was preventing the ship from setting sail. The rope was frayed and the last strand needed to be cut. We prayed that whatever that rope represented would be released. Another picture was of a hawk hovering almost motionless. Suddenly it dived, right on target and secured its

prey. It seemed that the housing situation had been motionless
but suddenly God would act.

The conference was an exceedingly good one. Originally a
vision given to Michael Harper, it proved to be a time of great
blessing. The quality of the speakers was exceptionally high,
with powerful addresses from both the Archbishop of Cape
Town and Everett Fulham, an American Episcopalian who
spoke of the Spirit as the breath of the Lord that brings death
to what is not of God as well as life to those who are open to
Him.

The conference was a very busy one. Gathered together were
so many friends, who had shown me such love and kindness
during my travels to different parts of the world. It was good
to catch up on news and to share a vision of what God was
saying and doing in different places. There was little time to
think about the need of a house.

I had the joy of leading a seminar on "Renewal and Revival"
with Bishop Festo Kivengere from Uganda, at that time exiled
from his diocese. He is such a gracious and loving man and
I learned much from his long experience of the revival in East
Africa.

However, I had to spend the whole conference knowing that
I was to give the final address at the closing Eucharist in
Canterbury Cathedral. It was expected that God would have
something prophetic to say and I needed to be open to the Lord
to allow the Spirit to speak through me.

It proved to be a truly memorable service. In the vestry
beforehand I had the unique experience of having hands laid
on me by thirty bishops. What an incentive for any preacher!

The service ended with the bishops and myself dancing
around the high altar of the cathedral. For months afterwards,
no matter where I travelled in the world, I had to live with the
photograph of the Archbishop of Cape Town (the celebrant) and
myself holding hands in our robes while we danced with others
in praise of the Lord.

Witnessing the scenes was a visitor who had strayed into the cathedral to look around. She obviously could not believe her eyes and asked one of the vergers what was happening. "This is an Anglican Communion service," she was told. "Oh, no, it is not," she replied; "I am Anglican and this is definitely not an Anglican Communion service!"

The leaders' conference was followed immediately by an open conference. The numbers swelled from about 350 to approximately 1,500. Groups had flown in from many nations around the world, with jets being chartered for groups from the U.S.A. and Canada.

I had been asked to share a seminar with Bishop Bill Frey from Colorado on "The Church as a Community". Bill Frey is a lovely man of God and heads a community in his own diocese, which I was to visit later. There was such accord as we shared from the Scriptures together about what it means to be committed to one another in love. At the final service we all prayed fervently for the bishops in our midst who would be attending the Lambeth Conference itself, that God would give them opportunities to lead others into a new freedom in the Holy Spirit.

It was at the weekend conference that the matter of our needing a house was raised once again. Someone had heard from someone else, who had heard from someone else that there was someone at the conference who had recently inherited a house and wanted it used for Christian purposes. The last links in the chain were Michael and Jeanne Harper.

Michael and I established contact with Michael Warren and his wife Gillie. It transpired that about a year previously Michael's mother had died, leaving an estate in Sussex to his sister, Mary, and himself. The estate was managed on their behalf, and they wanted the main house used for the Lord's purposes. Their first thought was to make it a Christian Conference Centre. The Lord had prevented that, telling them that he had some particular use for it. At the right time he would send the right people to them. Meanwhile they were to keep the place ready for use. The furniture was not put under dust sheets; instead the house was kept dusted, cleaned and heated, ready for occupation.

But by whom? Us? Perhaps. The Warrens did not want to make any hasty decisions; neither did we. We had visited large houses before and knew nothing about the details of this one, except that it had been described by Michael Warren as "a pleasant house".

It so happened that the members of the family had arranged to meet at the house, called "The Hyde", on the following Thursday. They had sensed that the Lord was wanting them to make a decision about its use. It was decided on the Sunday, the last day of the Canterbury Conference, that Caroline and I would join the family at that meeting.

During those next four days, I knew that this was the place, this was God's answer. The others in the household shared this conviction. Perhaps at last I would have an answer to the children's continual question: "Where are we moving to?"

We had been warned that The Hyde was a little inaccessible, and so it proved; Caroline and I arrived late for the appointment. "Private drive to The Hyde" the notice by the gate had said. For over a mile the road wound on through beautiful woodland, until there, at last, was a pair of wrought iron gates. We drove on between high rhododendron bushes and suddenly we were being greeted by Michael Warren and introduced to Mary and Kenneth Habersham. They had been waiting outside for us.

We were ushered into the drawingroom before we had a chance to look at the exterior of the building. Within two hours it was settled. We all had the witness that this was the place God intended for us. Legal formalities would have to be dealt with in due course. It was July 21st. On August 30th we would move into The Hyde.

"Welcome to your new home," Michael Warren said. "Now you'd better come and see what you are getting."

All this had been decided before Caroline and I saw over the house. That was probably just as well, for when we did we were bemused. The Hyde was originally a hunting-lodge build in the mid eighteenth century and extended into a fine country house in 1842. It is a good size, without being enormous like the houses we had seen in recent months. The rooms are generous in their proportions and beautifully furnished.

Everything was in place to the last teaspoon. The Lord had meant what He said: we would need to bring nothing with us. We would be able to move and continue to apply ourselves whole-heartedly to the ministry, without having to see a house rebuilt around us.

When we toured the grounds we were equally amazed. Half of the twenty-eight acres were laid out in carefully planned formal gardens; the rest was beautiful parkland leading down to two lakes. It was all bewildering.

We returned home scarcely knowing how we could describe our new home to the others. It was as well that we had arranged to have a picnic at The Hyde with the Warrens a few days later, to enable our children, the household and David and Jane to see the place for themselves.

We were full of praise for the Lord's generosity and faithfulness. While writing *Anything You Ask* I had sensed the Lord was going to put this teaching on faith to the rest. Little did we expect all this. But it had been worth it. Much had happened to all of us spiritually during the course of these months of waiting on the Lord. God had given us faith for the future.

During the course of the year, other things had also happened to inspire faith. In May I had been in Canada. The tour began in the province of Manitoba and included a visit to the remote northern region. The distances people travel there are vast, one minister completing a round trip of 900 miles just to be at the afternoon leaders' meeting and evening service.

In Alberta, much of the ministry was centred on what it means to pray with faith. I was speaking on this subject one evening when suddenly there was a great commotion and people began rushing towards a man, whom I had noticed looking strange for some minutes. I did not realise that his heart had stopped beating. When his wife realised what had happened her cry of concern caused others to rush to her help. The man was a member of this particular congregation and had been released from hospital only a couple of weeks previously after suffering a serious heart attack.

None of this was known to me at the time. As far as I was concerned somebody had been taken seriously ill; but there was no need for anxiety. After all, we were in the process of looking at the Lord's teaching on praying with faith. I told everybody to quieten down, be at peace and pray with me.

A doctor and two nurses were present. They had laid the man on the floor. One of the nurses, who had considerable experience of working with heart patients, told me afterwards that there was no trace of a pulse.

As we prayed, the heart began to beat and the pulse returned. "That man was dead," she said, "and life came back into his body."

Someone had telephone for an ambulance knowing the seriousness of his condition. He was carried out on the stretcher fully conscious. When he was given detailed tests in hospital on the following day, there was no indication of any heart disorder. Nor was there any trace of damage caused by a previous heart attack. The doctor said that it was impossible that he could have suffered such an attack.

Praise our wonderful Lord, our healer. Since then I have heard that the man returned to work and a normal life.

Although I was not aware of the serious nature of the situation, the members of the congregation were. They had prayed for him throughout his previous stay in hospital. The Lord touched many others with His Spirit and healing power that evening.

From Alberta I went by coach through the Rockies to Vancouver. That two-day bus journey was unforgettable for its beauty and loneliness. It is at times like this that I miss my wife and children deeply. They will have to be with me next time I make such a journey.

From Vancouver I made a return visit to Victoria, again the guest of John Vickers, the retired priest who ran the Renewal Centre. People responded readily to the ministry and the Lord encouraged me personally.

John is a man of prayer and was one of those I asked to pray at Canterbury about the housing need. During the mission he prayed: "Lord, these have been days of such blessing it would be good to send Colin home with a really generous love-gift, say $1,000."

"Not a thousand dollars, John," the Lord replied, "a thousand pounds."

"But, Lord, that will mean an offering of over $1,400 tonight."

"That's right."

When he took me to the airport on the following morning, John handed me a bank draft for one thousand pounds and told me of his prayer conversation. At the meeting he had made no elaborate appeal at the offering; he had quietly expected the Lord to touch the hearts of people to release the amount he had specified. The love-offering yielded precisely the amount required.

All the money that comes through such gifts goes to the work of the ministry, and not to me personally. I was so moved by the Lord's generosity and thankful for John's faith. What a God! How faithful and full of love! No wonder Jesus was constantly encouraging us to have faith in Him.

8   Conflicting Reactions

"WHAT ARE WE doing in such a lovely place?" I had never expected such a privilege. The weather was beautiful during that first September at The Hyde. Every day was hot and sunny and each morning I woke up bewildered to be in such surroundings. The Lord must have some important reason for our living here.

It was several months before I could refer to the house as "home"; it was always "The Hyde" in conversation. Learning to live there was a slow process.

This would be an ideal place for leaders to receive ministry, but the community would need to develop further before this could happen effectively. However, a steady stream of visitors began as soon as we had moved. People wanted to see this beautiful place for themselves, and hear about the gracious way in which the Lord had provided it.

Not that I had much time to settle in; within a few weeks I was flying to Toronto for a three-week mission to the diocese. Ridley and Madge Williams had become firm friends since my first visit to Toronto and had been visiting us when we took the children for the picnic at The Hyde to show them their new home.

Ridley, a member of the Diocesan Renewal Committee, not only provided me with hospitality, but also accompanied me throughout this time of ministry. The schedule was extremely busy: every opportunity to promote renewal within churches was to be gratefully received and used.

Once again I was the guest speaker at the Diocesan Renewal Conference, which began with a Eucharist in the cathedral at which the bishop presided. The Lord moved powerfully and the people were still praising Him at eleven p.m. The bishop then announced from the steps of the high altar: "It's time to go home." He promptly gave the blessing and we processed into the vestry. The people went on singing the Lord's praises.

In the vestry the bishop, for whom I have always had a deep respect, said "Boy, that was great; but enough is enough!" I went back into the church and joined in the praise!

I was preparing for the first conference session on the following morning when I heard a female voice singing a most anointed song: "Feeling the Spirit of the Lord". I could not resist going into the hall to see who was singing.

Later I met Ruth Fazal. She had been at the conference two years previously and God had really spoken to her through the ministry then. She had written several songs, which encapsulated the teaching that I had given. She led much of the worship at this conference and also in several other places where I spoke as I toured around the diocese. Each time she produced another new song arising from the previous teaching session — truly a great gift which complemented the ministry of the Word. Later Ruth was to minister with us in England.

August, instead of being the usual holiday period, had been taken up with conferences and the business of moving house. It was the Lord's grace, together with Ridley's great encouragement, that kept me going during my time in Toronto. The over-busy schedule meant that I was renewing my battle with exhaustion, and again I was suffering physical pain as a result. Whenever I was ministering the Lord would graciously remove all the symptoms. As soon as I had finished, back they would all come. I was praying and believing for healing, but I knew clearly what God was saying; "You cannot go on treating your body the way you do." I had to hear the Lord in my physical limitations.

The last day before flying home was a Sunday. In the morning I was to preach at the service at Ridley's home church. I hardly slept on the Saturday night but was determined to fulfil my engagements on the Sunday. I had never cancelled an engagement, not even for health reasons, and I didn't intend to begin now. Somehow the Lord would carry me through.

I managed to get dressed and went downstairs with as good a mask as I could manage, but there was no disguising the way I felt. When I arrived at the church it was decided that I should sit quietly in the vestry until it was time to preach. Fortunately, the door from the vestry to the church was near the pulpit. I could slip discreetly into place at the right time.

I gripped the sides of the pulpit for support and began. Life and strength immediately flowed through my body. Apparently nobody was aware of anything being wrong, apart from the fact that I looked tired — something I was so used to people telling me. As soon as the sermon and time of prayer were finished I felt awful again. I went back to the vestry to wait for the next service. Once again the Lord supplied the necessary grace. He kept me going too for the evening service at St. John, Dixie, to the west of Toronto. I was deeply thankful for all the love Madge and Ridley showed me. Ridley felt guilty about the overbusy schedule, but I assured him that my condition was the cumulative effect of several months of intense activity.

When he took me to the airport, he told the checking-in clerk that I was not well, something I would never have admitted myself. Mercifully, I was placed alone in a row of three seats, enabling me to lie down for the duration of the flight.

We had to miss a scheduled stop en route to London because of bad weather, so we landed early at Heathrow. The family had not yet arrived to meet me. The Lord was certainly dealing with any temptation to feel sorry for myself. By the time I arrived home I was in so much pain I didn't know where to put myself. We prayed and the Lord gave me sleep. And how I slept over the next few days.

"You must have a holiday" — everybody was insistent. I knew I had done it again. After that enforced holiday in Spain two years previously I had been determined never to get into a similar state of fatigue. Now here I was in a worse state than ever. I felt guilty and the last thing I deserved was a holiday.

"You must, you cannot go on like this." Now David and Jane added their voices. "You must go and lie in the sun somewhere," they all insisted.

"What, in December?" I retorted. "Anyway, it's impossible. I have engagements throughout the month."

"Then cancel them."

"No. I have never done that and I don't intend to start now!"

"Don't let pride get in the way." That made me think! "Besides, look at your schedule for next year. You will be forced to rest if you don't obey the Lord now and take one." That made me think still further. I knew in my heart that what they said was true.

In the event, we arranged for the whole family to go to the Canary Islands. I dragged myself through my November engagements in a cloak of tiredness and then headed for the sun. I had to cancel only three engagements in December to make the trip possible.

The children's school teachers were most encouraging when we inquired if it would be detrimental to their progress to take them away from school. Two weeks with their father would do them far more good, I was told. And besides, there would not be much academic work done at the end of the Christmas term.

That turned out to be one of the best holidays we have ever had. The children were most understanding and undemanding. Much time was spent sleeping, although there were plenty of opportunities for swimming, a favourite pastime of our younger daughter, Andrea. The highlight was undoubtedly an all-day donkey safari to a "lost village", only accessible by a track that went up the side of a mountain and down into a valley beyond. My heart was in my mouth on a number of occasions. Claire's donkey had the habit of straying to the edge of the track and looking over the precipitous drop. One step further and they would have fallen many hundreds of feet. Fortunately the donkey valued its own life as much as we valued Claire's.

*

Anything You Ask had been published a few weeks before we left for the holiday. After a year's ministry in which faith had been the keynote I knew how much such teaching was needed. And yet I was faced with a personal dilemma as a result of writing the book.

Eleven years previously the Lord had unexpectedly healed my eyes, an incident recorded in *When the Spirit Comes*. I had suffered from double vision when a child and it was a great joy to be able to dispense with glasses.

Earlier in the year I was becoming conscious of eye strain — not the former problem but a tiredness of the eyes. At first I took little notice, thinking that this was a symptom of general tiredness. However, with the intense concentration of writing *Anything You Ask* the eye strain increased. I prayed persistently about this but there was little improvement. When I came back from Canada I could ignore the symptoms no longer.

"Lord Jesus, please heal my eyes."

"What do you mean by that?" He asked me.

"Well, Lord, I want to be able to see clearly without any strain to my eyes."

"Go and get some glasses; then you will be able to see clearly and without strain."

I was stunned. I had not expected such an answer. How could I be sure that I was hearing the Lord aright? I decided to telephone the optician for an appointment for that same day; if this was really the Lord He would have to make that possible. At two p.m. my eyes were being examined.

It was suggested that I must have had surgery for the previous fault to be corrected. Only from the heavenly surgeon! However, I now needed glasses, especially for reading and writing. They were duly ordered.

I was in turmoil. The healing of my eyes eleven years previously was public knowledge. It would surely be dishonouring to the Lord for people to see me with glasses again! I was determined that I would not disguise the need by wearing contact lenses; that would not be honourable either.

Moreover, I had just written a book on faith. Where was my

faith now? In that book was teaching on the Lord's desire to heal, and here was I clearly in need of healing. Ironically, there continued to be a steady increase in the amount of healing taking place in my ministry. How could I pray with integrity for the sick while wearing glasses?

Perhaps I was over-sensitive. But my greatest concern was that the Lord should in no way be dishonoured. While I was waiting for the glasses to arrive, I was also waiting on the Lord. "Why Lord? What purpose will this serve?"

"It will demonstrate to everyone that the healing comes from me, not from you." He reminded me that many of the people who had been greatly used in the healing ministry needed healing themselves. He ministered His supernatural power through weak human vessels who themselves had obvious needs.

He further promised that I would see much more healing through my ministry in the future than I had seen in the past. That was to prove true. Further, He impressed upon me that there were many Christians spending too much time in seeking Him for things that were of little consequence. There was no sin in wearing glasses, so long as there was no lack of faith on my part in the healing grace of God. It would be a witness to others, He assured me, to concentrate on important issues.

By the time the glasses were ready for collection, I was reassured personally but I was still concerned about the reactions in others. I could anticipate the questions. "Why are you wearing glasses again?" "I thought God had healed your eyes?" "Why didn't your healing last?" And there would be all the unspoken questions as well!

I was relieved that many were too polite to put such questions to me personally. I had decided that it was better to say nothing, unless asked. I did not want to enter into any self-justification.

At first I needed the glasses for reading only, but soon became dependent on them. When the occasional question was asked I endeavoured to be as positive as possible in my response. And when people have come to testify that the Lord had healed their eyes during a meeting, I have rejoiced along with them. There has been one definite advantage; people cannot now see my eyes so clearly, and I am spared the persistent remark, "You do look tired."

After spending a few weeks at The Hyde, Maureen returned to New Zealand. She had been part of the music ministry on my first trip there. Her six-month stay had extended to an eighteen-month period and we were grateful for all that she had contributed to the ministry during that time.

It was great to have David and Jane with us; together with Vivienne, they were a real support to Caroline and the children, while I was away in Canada. If The Hyde was going to be used to the full, we would need more people to join us. Much work was involved in running such a large house, besides all the demands of the travelling ministry. The acre of kitchen garden was to remain unattended for many a month. Fortunately, the rest of the grounds were maintained in beautiful condition by the estate.

The Lord told us that He would supply people most suited to our needs. First, we must be patient. It was important to establish our life together as a small group, forming a firm foundation upon which He would then build. We were not to think of filling all the rooms with guests immediately and there was no need for us to feel guilty about living in such a house. In good time we would see it used to the full.

The expansion of the work that was beginning to take place made it advisable to form a charitable trust, known as the Bethany Fellowship. We had chosen the name "Bethany" for the ministry when we first left St. Hugh's. We wanted to avoid any personality cult and didn't want it to be known as "Colin Urquhart's ministry".

When praying about a name, it seemed that "Bethany" was appropriate. I was disappointed in a way because it did not seem a very imaginative title. But the Lord pointed out that:

1. Bethany was the place where Jesus' friends lived. He was assuring us of His love and that He wanted to come and make His home with us.

2. Bethany was the place where Lazarus was raised from the dead. Our ministry was to encourage resurrection in the churches; we were to bring men and women to new life in Jesus, as well as to encourage faith in His miracle-working power.

3. Bethany was the place where Jesus ascended to reign as King of glory. He was to reign as King in our lives and in this ministry.

In January 1979, Ginny Cox, who had been trained as an opera singer, joined us at The Hyde. With David and Vivienne often travelling with me, she would provide much-needed support at home.

As I look at the diary for the early months of that year, it strikes me that I was exceedingly slow in learning how to arrange my programme. It was a ceaseless whirl of travelling to many parts of England. However, it began with a real victory in prayer.

The post-Christmas period brought a heavy fall of snow. On January 3rd I was due to be speaking at Plymouth in Devon, a journey of well over 200 miles from The Hyde. The roads in some parts were barely passable on the previous day and in the early morning news bulletin on the 3rd there was a warning that an extremely strong blizzard was blowing across the Atlantic and would hit south Devon during the day.

The organisers of the meeting also heard this forecast and immediately telephoned us. The roads in Devon were already very bad. Any further fall of snow would make them impassable. They would understand if I did not want to make the journey. Even if we did arrive, local traffic would come to a standstill if the blizzard arrived.

We had already prayed before the telephone call and believed it right to travel. Our God was capable of intervening and changing the weather. I suggested to our brethren in Devon that they prayed and believed that the meeting would go ahead as planned.

We began what proved to be a long tortuous journey. There were places that were almost impassable, but not quite. We listened to the regular news bulletins and heard of the relentless course of this blizzard as it drew nearer to our shores. We continued to praise the Lord for His victory over the weather and confessed our faith that He would prevent that blizzard from hitting the south coast. Even with our mixture of weather in this country, it was most unusual to have the progress of a storm plotted in this way and reported on the news bulletins. But this was one of particular ferocity.

The newspapers the following morning flashed banner headlines about the mystery of this freak storm that had been heading for south Devon and at the last moment had veered southwards to hit northern France instead. It was inexplicable that it should take that particular direction and for no apparent reason. We didn't bother to inform the papers about what had happened; our explanation would probably not have been accepted.

The meeting went ahead as planned. The hall was packed to capacity, with people sitting around me on the platform as I spoke. Obviously the Lord had wanted that meeting to take place and all these people to be present. It was not only our prayers that had prevailed. We heard of the way many had been praying the blizzard away throughout the day in Plymouth and in Exeter where we were to minister afterwards. The whole episode was a great encouragement to faith.

Many Christians experience the longing to see relatives coming to the Lord. My younger brother and I were very different by nature. He was a successful and worldly businessman by the time of his third marriage. He had been a nominal churchgoer until the break-up of his first marriage, but had never known a personal relationship with the Lord Jesus. We saw very little of each other, had little in common and both led busy lives, although of a very different nature.

Our children dreaded visits from their Uncle Barry. To him, children were a nuisance and he let them know it. After one particularly trying occasion, our son Clive felt hurt and resentful for being made to feel unwanted.

"What do you think Uncle Barry needs?" we asked him.

"He needs to know Jesus," Clive was quick to reply. "If he knew Jesus he wouldn't be like this."

"Well, you had better forgive him and start praying for him; pray that he will come to know the Lord and will be given a new heart."

Clive took this advice. Every night he prayed for Barry and his wife, Sue. And every night for two years he thanked the Lord for bringing them into His Kingdom. "Believe that you have received it, and it will be yours!" A real object lesson in faith for a young boy, learning what it means to pray by faith with patience.

One day while I was away from home Barry called at The Hyde. *Anything You Ask* had just been published and Caroline felt it right to give him a copy as he was leaving. For some weeks it lay around his home unread. Then the crisis came, the crisis that seems to be necessary for many people before they feel desperate enough to turn to the Lord. Sue was in hospital because of a miscarriage and was not at all well. Barry picked up the book and began to read.

A few days later I received a telephone call from him. He sounded different, less confident of himself. "I think something has happened to me," he said. He then went on to tell me that when he reached Chapter Eight, which explains how to repent, give your life to Jesus and know His forgiveness, he had followed the advice given and had written a letter to Jesus. He had also read the following chapter about being baptised in the Holy Spirit.

"I think I need you to come and pray with me," he said. It so happened that I would be passing near his home on the following morning, so I arranged to call and see him then. I found him already humbled, as the Lord alone can humble a man. He was ready to enter the riches of eternal life in Jesus.

Barry prayed, giving himself to the Lord. Then I prayed with him to be filled with the Holy Spirit. Together we prayed for Sue. There was one important thing left for him to do.

"When you arrive at the hospital, tell Sue what you have just done. Tell her that Jesus is now your Lord and your Saviour."

"I don't know how she'll take that," he replied. "She won't understand what I mean."

I impressed upon him the importance of doing what the scriptures say: "If you confess with your mouth, 'Jesus is Lord', and believe in your heart that God raised him from the dead, you will be saved." (Rom. 10:9)

Later Sue told me that when Barry arrived at the hospital she was feeling very sorry for herself. Previously he had been all concern but, on this occasion, he walked into the ward with a broad beam on his face.

"What are you looking so happy about?" she challenged. Barry told her.

He was right, the news produced conflicting reactions within Sue. She made a good recovery and on returning home soon saw the radical changes in Barry. She began to read *Anything You Ask* — and followed the instructions of Chapter Eight and read Chapter Nine. I received another telephone call from my brother.

"Sue's ready. You had better come and pray with her."

And what a joy that was. Barry had known the Lord for only five weeks. He had made it a matter of intense prayer that Sue join him in the faith speedily. Sue, for her part, had been very sensible.

"I could see the changes in Barry," she said, "and I could tell that the Lord was now real for him. Did I really want Jesus myself? That was the question I had to face. I realised that it would be no good giving my life to God for Barry's sake or because of what had happened to him. My motives had to be right. I had to be sure that I meant what I was saying — that I was prepared to give my life to Jesus."

Sue was filled with the Holy Spirit and the two of them were one in Jesus. But that is not all. From the moment that Barry met with Jesus, his attitude towards the children changed completely. Clive's reaction to the news of Barry's conversion? "Jolly good job too!" Barry and he are now firm friends.

I had been moved by my son's persistent prayer. In fact he had put me to shame, for my prayer for my brother and sister-in-law had been by no means so faithful.

In the past three years they have continued to grow in the Lord and have needed to learn one lesson in particular. "The measure you give is the measure that you get back." This is a principle that Jesus reiterated in several different ways. It is true of relationships, forgiveness, attitudes and material possessions. God promises that He will give "good measure, pressed down, shaken together and running over" when we have given first. That is often where the step of faith is required.

There are many ways in which Jesus urges this principle of giving upon us:

Blessed are the merciful, for they will be shown mercy. (Matt. 5:7)

Give to the one who asks you, and do not turn away from the one who wants to borrow from you. (Matt. 5:42)

Love your enemies and pray for those who persecute you. (Matt. 5:44)

When you give to the needy, do not announce it with trumpets. (Matt. 6:2)

For if you forgive men when they sin against you, your heavenly Father will also forgive you. But if you do not forgive men their sins, your Father will not forgive your sins. (Matt. 6:14–15)

Seek first his kingdom and his righteousness, and all these things will be given to you as well. (Matt. 6:33)

Do not judge, or you too will be judged. For in the same way you judge others, you will be judged, and with the measure you use, it will be measured to you. (Matt. 7:1–2)

In everything, do to others what you would have them do to you. (Matt. 7:12)

When things do not appear to be going well, we are tempted to adopt the attitude: "Lord, you give to me first and then I shall have something to give back to you." The temptation when things are not good financially, is either to reduce your giving to the Lord and others, or to stop giving altogether. That is spiritually disastrous. The Lord has taught us to look to Him for the necessary provision for this ministry, but He has taught us the importance of giving. We can only expect the Lord to be supplying the "good measure, pressed down, shaken together and running over" if we are being faithful in our giving to others.

Barry is an architect. The recent recession was creating a crisis in the building industry and many architects were being made redundant. Work was hard to find, especially for those in small private practices such as his. He needed some help in knowing how to pray about the situation, and so came to see David.

David outlined the principles of giving to Barry, and he and Sue began to put them into operation. Their business began to thrive and prosper although the recession was growing worse. First they had to take on more staff, then extend their offices and then move to bigger ones. Throughout this process they continued to give generously to the Lord. As He caused them to prosper so they could give much more away for the work of the Kingdom.

This matter of giving is an aspect of faith that many Christians ignore. They do not appreciate sufficiently that the way in which we give is a test of our trust in the Lord and our faith in Him to measure back to us what we need. It is an indication of whether or not we believe in the faithfulness of God to fulfil the promises of His Word.

Jesus commended the poor widow for putting her last mite into the temple treasury. He commended her for the faith that she was demonstrating. That coin represented all she had, but she did not cling onto it. She gave it to her Lord trusting Him to care for her.

That, friends, is a demonstration of faith for the future.

9   Kingdom Authority

"THERE MUST BE an answer," I thought to myself. For some months I had been preaching about various aspects of faith, especially in relation to prayer and our daily lives. Faith includes having a positive attitude in the midst of adverse circumstances because God has made His resources available.

Everywhere I travelled I was aware of negative attitudes. In conversation many faithless statements would be made and unbelieving attitudes betrayed. At the end of meetings, people frequently came to share with me their tales of woe in ways which exhibited that they felt utterly defeated.

Even when people are brought to a new place of faith, how can that level of faith be maintained without sinking back into negative and defeatist attitudes? There must be a way, and the Lord was the only one to reveal the answer.

Jesus told His disciples: "Abide in me and I in you." (John: 15:4 R.S.V.) Paul repeatedly speaks of Christians living "in Christ Jesus". John talks about believers being "in God". What do such phrases mean? How can we abide in Him? What does it mean to live "in Christ Jesus"?

Emphasis on the indwelling presence of the Holy Spirit has brought many to a new appreciation of the truth that God lives in them. What does it mean to say that we live in God? If we are to live "in Christ Jesus" we obviously cannot live in pessimism, failure and defeat.

Some Christians experience a total change in their lives as

a result of turning to Christ. My brother was a good example of that. For others, there is not such an obvious transformation; they seemed to be battling constantly with the past. Why? Part of the answer revolves around repentance. Those who are led to a full and thorough repentance at the time of their commitment to Christ are liberated far more fully than those who are asked only to make some token act of repentance. "Asking Jesus into your heart" is no substitute for the Lord's command to repent, or His clear teaching that "If anyone would come after me, he must deny himself and take up his cross and follow me." (Matt. 16:24)

It is important to apply Paul's teaching about being dead to the old life. "For you died, and your life is now hidden with Christ in God." (Col. 3:3) Many of our problems and inner conflicts as Christians would not defeat us if we believed Paul's teaching: "For we know that our old self was crucified with him so that the body of sin might be rendered powerless, that we should no longer be slaves to sin — because anyone who has died has been freed from sin." (Rom. 6:6–7) As Christians we are to count ourselves "dead to sin but alive to God in Christ Jesus" (Rom. 6:11)

Paul is saying that we must reckon ourselves dead to sin, to our former way of life, and know that the power of sin is broken in our lives. Because we have been made new creatures, our lives are now hidden with Christ *in God*, we are "alive to God in Christ Jesus".

We are to see ourselves no longer living in sin, but in Him; no longer bound by the guilt and fear of the past but alive in Christ. He wants us to be living in the power of the new nature that He has given us — not to be wallowing around constantly in the past thinking that we are still bound by the old nature. Jesus died to set us free from that and we must not deny the power of His cross in our lives. How can we learn to live more effectively in the power of that new nature? How can others be taught and encouraged to do that?

"All that is not of faith is sin." Despite the new attitude to the life of faith, many of my thoughts and attitudes were still negative. I would have to allow God to deal with my negative attitudes if I was going to be able to teach others to be positive, and the community needed to be a corporate expression of what it means to live "in Christ Jesus".

I turned to the Scriptures to see what they taught about being in Him and saw that they gave me a portrait of my new life in Jesus. Several of my attitudes were inconsistent with such truths. My speech did not always agree with what God said about me in His Word as His child living "in Christ Jesus". If my attitudes and words disagreed with those of the Lord, someone had to be wrong — and it wasn't the Lord!

There was the nub of the problem. We Christians so often see ourselves through our own feelings, fears, doubts, insecurities, instead of seeing ourselves as God sees us. "But you were washed, you were sanctified, you were justified in the name of the Lord Jesus Christ and by the Spirit of our God." (1 Cor. 6:11)

I partially believed this portrait; I needed to believe it totally. Then I could communicate to others that if they were "in Christ Jesus", they too could believe all these truths about themselves.

The others in the community received all this as good news. Each of us began to search the New Testament to build up the portrait that God gives us there of our new life in Christ Jesus. We recognised that our thinking, attitudes and speaking needed to be consistent with these truths at all times. We had to ask the Lord to forgive our negative attitudes of the past and prayed for the Holy Spirit to witness these truths of God's Word in our hearts, and to give us the grace to speak them out in every situation. It was important not only to believe the Word, but also to confess it, to speak it out.

In this we could help and encourage one another. We agreed to correct each other (lovingly!) whenever we spoke or betrayed negative, unbelieving attitudes. If anybody was obviously feeling sorry for himself and had taken his eyes off his faith picture of his new life in Jesus, he could have his attention redirected to the Lord.

At first we were correcting each other constantly, often with considerable humour. It was amazing to realise how many negative reactions were going on within us, totally unrecognised. The revelation of what it means to be "in Christ Jesus" became more real for all of us. We readily responded to our need to see ourselves as God sees us and to speak of ourselves accordingly.

Within weeks the change within the members of the community was apparent. Two or three who had oversized inferiority feelings and negative attitudes towards themselves were particularly helped. They had received much counsel and advice from various people over the years, but without a great deal of effect. Now the Word of God was doing the work within them. No wonder Jesus said: "My words are spirit and life."

I was explaining to one gathering how we had learned to check each other of negative reactions and to point each other back to Jesus and the truth of the new life that we have in Him. After the meeting, David said to me: "Do you realise that we hardly ever have to correct each other now?" This was true; our thinking and speech had become far more positive and faith-full.

Since then we have had to learn to continue affirming positively who we are in Jesus, and not allow adverse circumstances or feelings to draw us away from the truth. As we have a steady flow of people joining the community, we have to reiterate this teaching and encourage them into a new place of faith. It is great to see the changes that happen to people as a result.

These truths have also affected our ministry to others. There are many who are sent to us in great need. David and others have learned how to direct them to the truths of Scripture; to show them how they are dead to the old life and can now be free to live the new life they have been given "in Christ Jesus".

We know that we live in Him and He in us, because He has given us of His Spirit. (1 John 4:13)
If anyone acknowledges (confesses or speaks out) that Jesus is the Son of God, God lives in Him and He in God. (1 John 4:15)

David Brown was continuing to be a great encouragement to me. He travelled nearly everywhere with me and, having a beautiful humble spirit, was content to listen and learn. He took careful note of how to minister to people both collectively and individually, and agreed with me in prayer concerning every aspect of our community life and ministry. I have met few people that are as quick to comprehend spiritual truths and as ready to respond to them. As a result he learned rapidly and was maturing steadily in his faith in Jesus and the life of the Holy Spirit.

He had one big difficulty: he was too nice! That might seem a strange thing to say; but when counselling people, a positive and direct word often needs to be spoken to them to lead them to repentance and amendment of life. David could often see what needed to be said, but couldn't bring himself to say it.

Slowly this fault was corrected. As a result he is positive and direct in his dealing with people, but has lost none of his graciousness. It is not loving to be soft with people; neither is it loving to be hard. Those with emotional difficulties need someone who is strong and positive, who won't "let them off the hook" or allow them to avoid the issues they need to face honestly.

The disciples learned from Jesus "in the field" or "on the job". He sat them down and taught them; but much of what they learned about faith and ministry came from watching the Master at work, seeing Him heal the sick, cleanse the lepers, cast out demons, raise the dead and perform miracles. And Jesus sent them out to do likewise: "Freely you have received, freely give."

David was happy to learn in that kind of way and the result is that now he has a strong and powerful ministry. There is an obvious anointing from God upon His life and the Lord's authority is evident in both his preaching and leadership.

Wherever David and I travelled we saw the Lord at work. Caroline and the others at home had always been frustrated by my lack of communication about what happened on ministry trips; I never knew what to say. It was incredibly difficult to put into words the way in which the Holy Spirit was at work at meetings. I did not want to take any glory for myself by even talking about what He had done.

Also I had learned not to judge meetings. People often asked me: "Was that a good meeting?" "Were you satisfied with the response?" I would always be evasive in my answers. As far as I was concerned, I had to be sensitive to the leading of the Spirit and obedient to the Lord in speaking whatever words He gave me to speak, and in ministering in whatever way He was leading. I could do no more than that; I had to leave the outcome to Him. It was not for me to judge Him or the moving of His Spirit. But it was my responsibility to ensure that I was in the right place with Him, not only at the time of speaking, but in every aspect of my life. Only then would He work through me in the way that He desired.

Of course, I was aware of great things happening to people; and yet, in a strange sense, that had nothing to do with me. And so my comments on returning home would usually be so general as to be infuriating to the others: "Oh, the Lord was at work." "Yes, He was busy." "Yes, there were a lot there." "He's a mighty God, so of course He did mighty things."

I was constantly being urged to be more specific when writing the circular letters to our prayer partners. As I have read through them in preparation for this book, I see them filled with these general statements. Now that David was travelling with me I could leave the explanations to him. He had a pet phrase: "That was something special." He soon discovered that this was as infuriating as my generalities and learned to be more specific.

There was also another reaction within me. When I came home I wanted to relax with my family and the community, to "switch off" for a few hours and be relieved of the pressures of ministry.

In July, David came with me on a trip to Switzerland and France. We decided that it would be simpler and cheaper to travel by car. While driving through France to Montreux, on the shore of Lake Geneva, the gear box jammed in second gear. It was impossible to shift it and there was little time to spare if we were to arrive at our destination on time. There was only one thing to do. We pulled into the side of the road and prayed the prayer of faith: "Believe that you have received it and it will be yours."

We tried the gear stick; it was still immovable. Faith is what you do, not simply what you say. "Let's go," I said to David. "We believe we have the answer, so we don't have to stay stuck here."

We set off in second gear, praising the Lord for His victory. A few hundred yards down the road, the gear box suddenly freed and we had no further trouble.

Over the years we have known the Lord intervene on several occasions when a mechanic has been needed. When I was away from home one weekend, Caroline took the children to Luton to visit friends there. They left early on the Sunday morning to ensure arriving in time for the service at St. Hugh's.

On the motorway the car began to misfire. Caroline encouraged the children to praise the Lord with her. As they began to sing, the car engine ran normally. Whenever they stopped praising it would begin to misfire again. That encouraged their singing! The hard shoulder of the M1 is the last place to be stuck with three children on a Sunday morning. By the time they arrived at St. Hugh's they had already had their own worship service in the car. They parked and hurried into the service.

Afterwards a mechanic friend looked at the engine and immediately saw the problem. "How did you get the car here?" he asked Caroline.

"I drove it here, of course," she answered.

"You can't have done," he replied. "It is totally impossible for this engine to run because the distributor lead is broken."

"All things are possible for our God."

Perhaps our most amazing motoring incident took place while towing our caravan to Canterbury for a family camp. The caravan tyre was punctured on a heavily cambered road, which made it extremely difficult to jack it up properly. I managed to remove the wheel, but the tyre was useless. I found a dealer and had a new tyre fitted but, on returning to the caravan, found the wheel with the inflated tyre impossible to refit. The caravan could not be raised further.

I was speaking at the opening meeting that evening and we had been praying that the delay would not make us late. Suddenly a car drove straight up to us, a young man got out and said, "Let me do this for you." From the boot of his car he took a hydraulic jack, raised the caravan and fitted the wheel complete with the new tyre. He lowered the caravan, replaced the jack in his car and drove off *in the same direction from which he had come*! How did he know we were there? Who was he? Who had sent him?

There are some questions that remain unresolved. I am sure Jesus is well aware of all the answers.

From Montreux, Switzerland, David and I drove to Chalon-sur-Sâone. There at a Bible College, La Porte Ouverte, a national, ecumenical, charismatic conference is held each year presided over by Thomas Roberts, a Welshman who has spent much of his long life in France. He is greatly loved and respected by the French people and has a profound effect there upon ecumenical relationships and the charismatic renewal.

As part of the ministry, I was asked to lead the healing service on the Sunday afternoon. The 1,500 delegates were joined by others from the surrounding district. The teaching on faith had met with a ready response; and there was a great expectancy that God was going to work powerfully.

I had been particularly impressed by worship at the conference. Often, without any preliminaries, one of the leaders would begin a session by simply saying: "Let us worship God in the Spirit." Immediately the great congregation would burst into song, singing spontaneously in the Spirit to the glory of the Lord.

When it came to the time of ministry at the healing service, I knew that it was right to lay hands on people, although this was not my usual practice at such large gatherings. In France people expected the miraculous, but looked to personal ministry to effect that. The Lord was prepared to meet with people according to their faith.

That afternoon, together with David, I must have laid hands on 1,200 people or more. That took hours, and the congregation continued to praise the Lord throughout. Every time they saw a demonstrable healing take place they would burst out in applause, clapping the Lord with joy. Then they would flow naturally into singing in the Spirit and songs of praise until the next miracle. Some would come to the microphone and give testimony of what God had just done, while David and I went on praying with other folk.

The more they saw and the more testimonies they heard, the more people came for ministry. The entire service lasted for about five hours and we must have been praying with people for well over three of these. The worship continued throughout this time and was most inspiring. I have never been to a service quite like that before or since.

Of course, it had long overrun its time and there was only a short break for the evening meal before people were back in the vast tent again, worshipping the Lord in the scheduled Evangelistic Service. Those who know the French will realise how mightily God must have been moving for them to hurry a meal!

That whole conference was a great blessing to me and gave me a real love for the French people. When the Lord had made it clear to me that I was to leave St. Hugh's, He told me: "I will give you a love for all my people, as I have given you a love for the people here."

What a joy and a blessing it is to see God meeting with people in His sovereign power. You can never lose your sense of awe and wonder at the graciousness of our God, no matter how many people you see Him transform and heal. Neither can you ever become complacent. What God has done elsewhere on another occasion means little to people; they, and the Lord, are concerned about what is going to happen at this meeting.

There have been times when I have felt at the end of a service that I have grieved the Spirit by not obeying everything He was prompting me to do. For example, I was preaching at a morning service in Canada and there was a mighty anointing on the Word. I sensed that several would come into the Kingdom and that many needed to be baptised in the Holy Spirit. I knew also that another service followed hard on the heels of this one.

I think the Lord was wanting me to invite people forward for prayer. It was a large congregation and I was sure that the response would be great. There simply wasn't time. Instead I led a time of prayer encouraging people to receive the Lord and His Spirit where they were in their places. As I returned to my seat I knew that, although that was the right way to minister on many occasions, it hadn't been right this time.

"It's just as well you didn't have an altar call," the minister said to me after the service: "you would have had the entire congregation come forward." I couldn't escape from the fact that this was precisely what the Lord had intended. What about the service that followed immediately? What a witness it would have been to have seen the entire congregation at the earlier service seeking ministry. Perhaps the first service would have flowed on into the second.

Praise God that there is no condemnation for those who are in Christ Jesus! Whenever we make mistakes, He is ready to forgive us if we come to Him humbly, acknowledging our fault and asking Him for His pardon. Such mistakes make me more determined to obey what the Lord says in the future.

The experience of that healing service at La Porte Ouverte, great as it was, caused me to seek the Lord afresh. There must be a better way of ministering personally to people in a vast crowd, a way that would be as powerful as praying individually with folk, but much quicker. I still encouraged people to pray with one another, often joining hands as they did so, and believing that the power of God would flow through the entire gathering. But I knew how helpful it was to many folk to have some personal word from God to encourage their faith.

The Lord was not long in showing me the answer to my dilemma. About four weeks later I was the guest speaker at the Good News Crusade camp at Blaithwaite, at the invitation of Don Double. John Hutchison was the other guest speaker.

For some time I had been increasingly aware of specific things

God was doing at meetings, of someone being healed of a particular disease, or of the Lord meeting a person in a certain dilemma. At first I said nothing on such occasions, but quietly thanked the Lord that He was at work in such ways. Without any invitation from me, people would speak to me at the end of meetings, telling me exactly what had happened to them. They were greatly encouraged when I told them the Lord had made me aware of their healing; that served as confirmation for them. I was slow to use these words of knowledge in any other way.

The secret of having the Lord's authority in our lives and ministries is to be completely submitted to His authority and lordship. The more we are submitted to Him, the more of His authority is seen in us. People had often remarked to me on the note of authority in my preaching. That caused neither pride nor complacency, for I constantly recognised the need for more of the authority of Jesus in my ministry. Faith and the use of authority go together in the gospels and are seen supremely in the ministry of Jesus. His authority mastered every situation. I was only too aware of the many occasions when I had insufficient of the Lord's authority to see His victory in those particular circumstances. That caused me to seek the Lord still further, not so much for more of His power, but to be submitted completely to Him. I was not content with what I saw happening, but more concerned about what I didn't see taking place.

What had so often impressed me from the gospel accounts was that Jesus spoke the word and it was done; He truly spoke with authority. Instead of praying long prayers, He addressed the need:

"Be clean." Immediately he was cured of his leprosy. (Matt. 8:3)
"Go! It will be done just as you believed it would." And his servant was healed at that very hour. (Matt. 8:13)
Then He got up and rebuked the winds and the waves, and it was completely calm. (Matt. 8:26)
"Take heart, son; your sins are forgiven." (Matt. 9:2)

"Get up, take your mat and go home." And the man got up
and went home. (Matt. 9:6–7)
"Take heart, daughter," he said, "your faith has healed you."
And the woman was healed from that moment. (Matt. 9:22)
Then he touched their eyes and said, "According to your faith
will it be done to you," and their sight was restored.
(Matt. 9:29–30)

Didn't Jesus give authority to the disciples to act in His name?
"He called his twelve disciples to him and gave them authority
to drive out evil spirits and to cure every kind of disease and
sickness." (Matt. 10:11) Perhaps too often we ask the Lord to
heal, when He has given us the authority to heal in His name.
He commands the disciples: "Heal the sick, raise the dead,
cleanse those who have leprosy, drive out demons. Freely you
have received, freely give." (Matt. 10:8)

Because they were given authority by Jesus, they saw Him
at work when they acted in His name. "Then Peter said, 'Silver
or gold I do not have, but what I have I give you. In the name
of Jesus Christ of Nazareth, walk.' Taking him by the right hand,
he helped him up, and instantly the man's feet and ankles became
strong. He jumped to his feet and began to walk." (Acts 3:6–8)

There had been occasions when I had known the Lord's
authority to speak a word of healing and the deed was done.
A small boy who was going blind was an example of this. Could
this kind of ministry be exercised in a wider, and more public
setting? From the promptings that the Holy Spirit was giving
me it seemed that it could.

Don Double and John Hutchison were used to ministering
together and both were experienced in their use of the word
of knowledge, one of the gifts of the Holy Spirit mentions in
1 Corinthians 12. They spent time waiting on the Lord before
the evening meeting and He showed them specific needs that
would be met. When these words of knowledge were used during
the time of ministry, they were clearly accurate. God dealt with
people in a variety of ways, drawing them to repentance, expos-
ing and healing their needs.

Perhaps I should be bolder in the use of this spiritual gift. Perhaps I needed to wait upon the Lord for words of knowledge before the meeting. I decided to draw aside with the Lord to see if there was any witness from the Spirit that this was right for me.

When I did so I was amazed at how readily the Lord made me aware of what was to happen that evening. I knew that He wanted me to speak from John's First Epistle on what it means to love one another. It was almost unbelievable when He impressed upon me that there would be over a hundred people with a relationship of genuine hate for others in the fellowships to which they belonged. At the meeting I asked people to stand if they had such a hate relationship and immediately over a hundred people stood to their feet.

The Lord was encouraging me further in using the word of knowledge. However I must allow the Spirit to show me the way in which this gift was to be used in my particular ministry. There was no need to copy what I had seen in others, although He used that to give me more faith for the future.

"The Kingdom of God" was the theme of this particular camp. Just as I had needed revelation of what it meant to be "in Christ Jesus", I also needed revelation concerning the New Testament teaching on the Kingdom of God or the Kingdom of Heaven.

Over the years, the Holy Spirit has taken me on a conducted tour of the Scriptures, bringing to life one aspect of teaching after another. In preparation for this conference and the months of ministry that were to follow, the whole concept of the Kingdom came to life. All at once I realised that there were many Christians who had never received personal revelation in their hearts that they were part of God's Kingdom. They knew they belonged to Jesus and to His Church, but for most the Kingdom was regarded as something that happened to them in the future, beyond the grave.

There is a sense in Scripture in which the full manifestation of the Kingdom does lie in the future, and will only be seen on earth fully when Jesus comes again in glory. And yet the

Kingdom was the substance of the teaching of Jesus. He came proclaiming: "Repent, for the kingdom of heaven is near." (Matt. 4:17) With the coming of the King of heaven men were presented with the opportunity to enter the life of His Kingdom. The condition? Repentance. "Jesus went throughout Galilee, teaching in their synagogues, preaching the good news of the kingdom, and healing every disease and sickness among the people." (Matt. 4:23)

The signs and wonders were the evidence of the truth that Jesus proclaimed: the Kingdom of God was among men, within them, even, when their faith was in Him. He told the people to seek the Kingdom first in their lives. He taught them to pray: "Your kingdom come, your will be done on earth as it is in heaven." (Matt. 6:10) He made it clear that "Not everyone who says to me 'Lord, Lord', will enter the Kingdom of heaven, but only he who does the will of my Father who is in heaven." (Matt. 7:21)

He taught about the Kingdom in parables, such as: "The kingdom of heaven is like treasure hidden in a field. When a man found it, he hid it again, and then in his joy went and sold all that he had and bought that field. (Matt. 13:44)

To be a part of God's Kingdom is a privilege beyond price. To receive that revelation is like discovering the treasure hidden in a field. And Jesus had made clear the terms upon which men would make that discovery:

I tell you the truth, unless you change and become like little children you will never enter the kingdom of heaven. Therefore, whoever humbles himself like this child is the greatest in the kingdom of heaven. (Matt. 18:3–4)

It tell you the truth, unless a man is born again he cannot see the kingdom of God. (John 3:3)

I tell you the truth, unless a man is born of water and the Spirit, he cannot enter the kingdom of God. (John 3:5)

When Jesus sent His twelve disciples out, their message was to be His message, their ministries an extension of His own

ministry. The same was true for the greater number of disciples
that He sent out: "When you enter a town and are welcomed,
eat what is set before you. Heal the sick who are there and tell
them, 'The kingdom of God is near you'." (Luke 10:8, 9) And
they returned to Him, rejoicing at the things that they had seen
happening.

Jesus told them: "However, do not rejoice that the spirits
submit to you, but rejoice that your names are written in
heaven." (Luke 10:20) The reason for seeing God perform
mighty works was the real cause for joy, not the mighty works
themselves. To belong to Jesus is to have all the resources of
His Kingdom available to you.

For Paul, "The kingdom of God is not a matter of talk but
of power." In his ministry he was not content with teaching
about the Kingdom, he knew that the works of the Kingdom
must be demonstrated. If anybody is tempted to imagine that
the Kingdom was robbed of its power with the passing of the
apostolic age, he needs to heed the words of the commission
Jesus gave His disciples: "All authority in heaven and on earth
has been given to me. Therefore go and make disciples of all
nations, baptising them in the name of the Father and of the
Son and of the Holy Spirit, *and teaching them to obey everything
I have commanded you*. And surely I will be with you always
to the very end of the age." (Matt. 28:18–20 — italics mine)

We inherit those same commands that Jesus gave to His
disciples. He makes available the same power and authority to
His Church today as He did to His Church then. So much
hinges on knowing that this is yours as a child of the Kingdom.

It must be possible to speak to the mountains of need in
people's lives and command them to move in the name of Jesus.
Obviously this has to be done under the direction and anointing
of the Holy Spirit, for Jesus would not have acted in any other
way.

In the following weeks and months I became more conversant
with the word of knowledge ministry. Sometimes, before a
meeting, the Spirit of God indicated clearly specific things that
He wanted to do during the time of ministry. For example,

when travelling northwards for an evening meeting in Darlington, the name of a woman and her particular need was impressed upon me. Before preaching I asked the woman to come forward. She looked startled that God should have singled her out and addressed Himself to her need so specifically. I assured her that this was only because He wanted to heal her. When we prayed, the Lord met powerfully with her. The faith of the whole congregation was lifted and many other powerful works were done by the Lord for the glory of His name.

Of her own volition, the woman came to another meeting some distance away to testify how her life had completely changed from that moment.

More often, God would give me the word of knowledge within the meeting itself. On that same trip, I began a sermon with the words: "John, the Lord wants you to be ordained and there are several others whom God is calling to full-time ministry here tonight." Later in the service about twenty people stood to say that they had received such a call and afterwards John came to see me. He was a Pentecostal who felt that God was wanting him to be ordained in the Anglican Church. He could not understand this and only a few days earlier, unknown to me, had visited an Anglican minister to seek his advice. He was looking for some word of confirmation for his call and so the use of the word "ordained" was significant.

The words of knowledge usually come during the time of ministry following the preaching of the Word. Sometimes they relate to specific areas where forgiveness needs to be received or given to others; often they are concerned with particular healings that are happening. Some words of knowledge could relate to several people at the same time, others are more specific and refer to a particular individual.

It was clear that the use of this gift must not appear to be some kind of spiritual confidence trick. Even if I believe that these things are happening, how can that fact be verified? It does not require great insight to know that many present would be tempted to imagine that the whole thing was unreal.

To counter this, at the end of the time of ministry I ask

people to indicate if they have received specific healing through that time of ministry. Up go the hands, a demonstration to all that God has truly been at work. Usually I ask those who have raised their hands to come and give me a single sentence testimony of what God has done. They have to be brief because there are usually so many. Sometimes there are too many hands raised to make this practicable, although there have been occasions when I have listened to as many as 300 such testimonies. Some people have to leave before they are able to share their blessing and many of these write to us later to share what God has done.

At first, after preaching and ministering for two hours I found it physically and mentally demanding to listen to such testimonies. After intense concentration it is good to have time to unwind. But I found it such a blessing spiritually to hear what God had been doing; the blessing far outweighed the inconvenience.

Henry Lambert-Smith, a retired minister on the team of St. Michael's, York, was at a meeting in Truro. He wrote in the church magazine:

> That sermon roused everyone's faith and expectation. Then we were at prayer. Out of the blue Colin said, "Now, I want you all to stand and join hands. Yes, across the aisles as well, and pray silently for someone you know who needs healing."
>
> That pregnant silence lasted some time. Then God's answers began to come, Colin being given a "word of knowledge" each time.
>
> "Someone with a stomach ulcer has been healed." "Someone with breathing difficulty has been healed." And many more. Among them was "Someone who is partially deaf has been healed."
>
> I only realised seconds after that this someone could be ME. I thanked God, bewildered and not quite sure. Later I found Muriel and Don had also thought of me, so we prayed together and asked God to confirm the message. (Meanwhile I discarded my hearing aid and I have not needed it since.)

You can guess that we went every night after all this. On the Friday evening, the last service we could attend, a "word of knowledge" came. "This is to confirm that a deaf person has been healed."

THAT WAS GOD'S GRACIOUS BIRTHDAY GIFT TO ME. Can you wonder that I want to tell the world about it? That there is a song of gratitude in my heart to my lovely God and my Saviour?

And I believe that this was meant not simply as an encouragement for me, but for all of us. God is saying to us at this time: "Be on the watch! I am among you IN POWER. Expect more healings. Expect them for your sick friends, for YOURSELVES.

As people gave me their testimonies I began to enquire at what point the healing took place. Some were already aware that the healing was happening before the word of knowledge was spoken: it came as a word of confirmation to them. More often, the healing occurred as soon as the word of knowledge was spoken; sometimes in response to faith, at other times when people were not aware of their own need as they were busy praying for others. Some received the word by faith as a promise from God, but were not aware of an immediate release from the need.

It was clear that more people received immediate healing through this ministry than through the laying on of hands — and the whole process was quicker, an important factor for large evening meetings. That in no way discredits the laying on of hands. Jesus used that method as well as speaking the word of healing directly. And we must always be obedient to what the Spirit is saying; sometimes it is right to offer people individual prayer.

One of the most important factors in healing is the corporate faith of the congregation. God responds to the faith of His people. At a meeting where faith is high, the words of knowledge can flow almost faster than I can speak them. On another occasion there may be little expectancy and this is reflected in the hesitant way in which the healings come, or in which they begin. Sometimes the first few responses can raise the level of faith and then the healings begin to flow more freely. To keep things in proportion it needs to be realised that the actual time of healing represents only a small part of most of our meetings; perhaps ten minutes in a total of between two and two and a half hours.

Not all healings are physical; Jesus is the greatest psychiatrist. Within a few seconds He can reach into the deep recesses of a person's mind and set him free from some deep emotional hurt or crisis. Many words of knowledge relate to such needs and folk are set free from deep fears or feelings of rejection. One of the more remarkable examples happened while I was ministering in the U.S.A., and points to another aspect of faith. When speaking out words of knowledge I sometimes don't understand them myself. It can be somewhat disconcerting to have to speak out things that make little sense, and this was such an occasion.

The Spirit impressed upon me that there was someone who needed to be set free from a great fear of trains, because of something that had happened to him when a child. At the end of the meeting a man told me that his father had been a stationmaster at a remote place on the prairies. As a small boy he had the run of the station and knew the train crews and often would be treated to an ice-cream by one of them. One day, when only three or four years old, he was eating an ice when a young friend asked him where he could obtain one. The boy pointed to the other side of the track. To get there necessitated crawling between the coaches of the train that was stationary at the time. As the small lad was making his way to the other side the train began to move and he was killed.

The man who stood before me had lived with that memory ever since those early days of his childhood. He knew in his mind that it was not his fault, it was an accident; a child so young could not be responsible for another equally young. And yet guilt had dogged him ever since.

That evening God spoke to that man, assured him of forgiveness, set him free from guilt, and healed him of all his negative reactions to that incident. He could hardly believe that after all these years he could be set free from such a painful memory. That is what Jesus, our mighty Lord, had done for him.

10   Now I Can See

"THAT'S ENOUGH OF fowl's feet and chicken heads!" was David's assessment of the food in Singapore. For the first time, he was accompanying me on one of these intensive trips abroad. His tastes in food were very English and traditional.

It was exciting to see how the Spirit of God was moving in Singapore, especially among the Anglicans, led by their bishop, Chu Banit. The response to the teaching exposed the hunger in the hearts of the hundreds who gathered for services in the cathedral and around the diocese, many of them young people, newly converted from pagan religions.

Since the time that their bishop was baptised in the Holy Spirit many of the other clergy had sought His power in their lives. As a result there had been a considerable movement of evangelism. Canon James Wong came into the liberty of the Spirit at about the same time as the bishop. He had a congregation of almost a thousand praising young people and was founding a number of new congregations.

Every day he had fresh stories to tell from the previous night's adventures. After the services he went to the homes of new converts to help them remove all the signs of their previous heathen ancestor worship. This involved removing the altars and shrines erected for the worship of heathen deities, which are evil spirits. Some of the stories of these escapades were truly harrowing.

It was important to remove these objects of fear and superstition; the only one who gives true peace and freedom is the Lord Jesus Christ. One could not doubt the reality of the satanic forces that are evoked by the worship of these other so-called gods or spirits. Praise God that the power and authority of Jesus given to His children is far greater.

The cost of becoming a follower of Jesus, in a society where only a small minority are Christians, can be high. After death, Chinese parents expect their spirits to be worshipped by their children. Therefore if the children become Christians they are usually disowned by their parents, are blamed for all the difficulties their parents encounter and are put under tremendous pressure by relatives to return to their traditional ancestral worship. It takes resolute faith and courage to resist all these pressures and remain faithful to Jesus.

From our time in Singapore we learned much as well as having the joy of sharing the life and the love of Jesus with others with whom we experienced the unity that only the Holy Spirit can give.

When we arrived at Wellington, New Zealand, we were met by my dear friend Cecil Marshall. Fortunately he had arranged for us to stay in a beach cottage to recover from the journey and time change — and from the twenty-six meetings at which we had ministered in Singapore during the past week.

We spent a good part of the time sleeping, with a gentle game of beach cricket for exercise. Then it was back to work and a tour of several different parts of New Zealand. There we experienced similar frustrations to those in England. There were many lovely people who were being used greatly by the Lord, but the challenge of facing up to the corporate commitment, of which the New Testament speaks so clearly, is always the most difficult and crucial aspect of renewal.

For David the whole trip was a revelation. He discovered how rapidly one grows in one's own spiritual life when having to seek the Lord continuously over a period of several weeks. He also found that there were few opportunities to see much of the countries that we visited, but as he commented: "We have come to see the people, not the scenery."

The autumn of 1979 saw the first significant extension of the community at The Hyde. Charles and Joyce Sibthorpe joined us together with their five children. Charles had been responsible for the organising of the Mission to Cornwall two years earlier and had some experience of living by faith. It was the eyesight of their daughter that was miraculously preserved by the Lord, as explained in *Anything You Ask*.

Francis Pym, an Anglican priest, Marigold and their four children also joined us. The Sibthorpes lived in two cottages that were joined into one in the grounds of The Hyde; the Pyms came to live with us in the main house until a further cottage was available.

Suddenly there were a lot more people around, including many children. Twelve of us had laid a foundation in our first year at The Hyde and now our numbers had doubled.

Charles came with me to South Africa, in January. The principal reason for the visit was to speak at the 1980 South African Renewal Conference at Johannesburg. This had been hastily arranged and the speakers had received their invitations only a few weeks previously. Normally it would have been impossible for me to go at such short notice, but it so happened that the first part of January had been designated as a writing period. When I prayed about the matter, it seemed right for me to accept the invitation to speak at the conference. Later I discovered that the other speakers had similar stories to tell. It seemed that the Lord had made it possible for these men to gather from many different nations, and everyone sensed that He had some mighty important reasons for this.

The conference was in two parts; the first for about 3,500 leaders from all over southern Africa. On the second evening I gave the main address on "The Power of the Kindgom". I remember it being a serious message, but a faith-building one, as folk received the revelation that they were part of the King-dom, with all its resources made available to them. During the

time of repentance this vast multiracial audience was very quiet
and prayerful. God was obviously at work in the hearts of His
people.

I then said that we would pray for the power of God's Holy
Spirit to come upon us to enable us to live as His Kingdom
people. What happened next was awesome. One moment there
was complete silence; the next, thousands of voices were lifted
in exultant praise. They had all begun to sing at precisely
the same second. It seemed that the Holy Spirit had literally
descended at that instant. For some minutes the great throng
of people sang in the Spirit.

As the singing died away we moved into the time of healing.
The words of knowledge came rushing out one after another,
but were soon drowned by the praises of the people. God was
moving among us in sovereign power. There were far too many
healed to ask them to come and give personal testimonies. I
suggested that when folk saw me walking around the complex
of buildings, they could stop me to share what the Lord had
done for them. For the rest of the conference it proved impossible to move anywhere without being besieged by those wanting
to share their testimonies.

Behind me on the platform someone had been jumping up
and down and stamping his foot. The man had received healing
in his leg and was testing it out to make sure that the healing
was complete. Not everybody was aware of their healing immediately. Justice du Plessis, David's brother, was among
the speakers in the front row of the audience. When he arrived
home that evening, he removed his shoe and sock and prepared
to dress a bunion that had troubled him for several years. To
his joy, it had completely disappeared.

However, this was by no means the end of God's mighty
working at this conference; He had scarcely begun. During the
day there were a number of seminars taking place simul-
taneously. I spoke on two subjects: "The Kingdom of God and
the Christian Community", and "Praying with Faith".

About a thousand people came to the latter. At the last session
of this seminar I suggested that we put into operation what we

had heard, and prayed the prayer of faith as taught by Jesus. Time was very limited as schedules have to be observed at such conferences. After a brief time of repentance, people joined hands to pray for one another as we asked the healing power of God to sweep through that gathering. When I asked people to indicate what had happened to them at least three-quarters of those present, well over 700 people, raised an arm to show that they had received healing from the Lord — and that had taken place within about three or four minutes. Again my reaction was one of awe. I was used to seeing God work in mighty ways, but not quite like this!

Perhaps you think I should have been on top of the world as a result; but as I have already explained, when the Lord works in such ways you know very well that none of the glory is yours. He has chosen to work in a sovereign way for His glory. In a strange way, I feel almost detached from the whole scene, as if I am a spectator standing back and watching the Lord at work. That is the secret of ministry in the Spirit; not to let yourself get in the way, but to allow the Holy Spirit to have His way. Perhaps you may think that there would be a temptation to be proud at ministering at such meetings. Don't worry, God keeps me humble.

On the evening when the Spirit seemed to descend on the whole conference, I was asked at the end of the service to pray for a fourteen-year-old African boy who was in a serious condition with a brain tumour. He was thin and gangling as he sprawled across his mother's lap; he was already blind and deaf. His mother was in a desperate state and begged me to pray for him.

As I did so, I knew it was God's purpose to heal him, but there was no visible sign of improvement. All I could do was tell the dear woman that I was convinced it was the Lord's purpose to heal her son.

Far from ending the evening elated because of all that God had done, I felt defeated. If it was God's purpose to heal this boy, why hadn't the healing taken place? As always, I can praise God for what I see Him doing; but what really concerns me is what I do not see happening.

A few evenings later, a German-born evangelist, Reinhold Bonkke, was speaking at the evening meeting. He had a very powerful testimony which he shared on that occasion and the response was tremendous. This was the first service of the open part of the conference and people came forward in their hundreds — for salvation, to be baptised in the Holy Spirit, to be healed. They were ushered into a neighbouring building where they received ministry in groups according to need. The speakers were asked to go and make themselves available.

As I was leaving the hall I saw that boy again. He was walking beside his mother; he could both see and hear. My reactions were a mixture of joy for him, praise to the Lord, and immediate heart-searching within myself. I *knew* the Lord had given assurance that he was to be healed. But why didn't the healing happen when I prayed for him?

You can always try to justify yourself in such situations. You could say: "The previous occasion was not God's timing", or "It was in His purpose to use someone else", or "Your prayer was part of the process, and you had heard the Spirit aright in being convinced that the boy would be healed."

There is no doubt truth in all such statements, but that is not the point. What was God saying to me in all this? He did not delay long in showing me the answer. "There needs to be more power and authority in your ministry; you need to grow in faith." Yes, that was right, and I knew it. More seeking of the Lord was required. There can be no room for complacency in the ministry of the Holy Spirit. And while the seeking was continuing, God would continue to give me encouragement.

After the conference the speakers had been asked to undertake engagements in major centres in South Africa. First we were taken to a country hotel for what had been intended as a rest after a week of intensive ministry. In the event, it was hardly a rest, but a very powerful time of prayer and waiting on the Lord, as the speakers from around the world joined with South African leaders in praying for their nation.

The tour that followed involved travelling to seven different cities in a week from Durban to Pietermaritzburg, back to Johannesburg, then to the cathedral at Pretoria where scores came into the Kingdom, were filled with the Spirit and healed. In the evening I spoke at Andreas Lombard's Afrikaans-speaking Presbyterian church. Some 350 people were packed into the building, with a further 250 on the grass outside, listening by means of loudspeakers.

From there we moved to Cape Town, where the meeting was to be held in St. John's, Wynberg. It was estimated that there were about 1200 people packed in like sardines, twice as many as the building was intended to hold. Over 400 had to be turned away. This time there was no grass outside to sit on.

After the great time of ministry in Cape Town two years previously the service had an air of reunion about it. There was a tremendous sense of unity as the archbishop led the worship at the beginning of the meeting. But it was hot, the hottest evening of the summer, and with the building so overcrowded, my shirt rapidly changed colour as I began to speak. I tried to ignore the physical circumstances and the Spirit of God moved very powerfully. At the end of the meeting I was listening for over an hour to single-sentence testimonies of what He had done.

From Cape Town to Port Elizabeth and another crowded church for a powerful meeting. At the end of the meeting I received one of the most moving testimonies I have heard. It was very brief and to the point.

Before me stood a young woman in her early twenties. Tears were streaming down her face. "What has the Lord done for you tonight?" I asked her gently.

Through the tears she replied: "When I came to the meeting I was blind; and now I can see. God has healed me. I can see clearly, I can see you."

The healing was confirmed by the friends who had brought her to the meetings and who stood beside her radiant with joy. My only regret was that there was no time to obtain more details of the healing; there were so many others queueing to give their testimonies. Perhaps others were not as dramatic but every healing is important. If God touches your life to heal even a minor ailment it is a great privilege and honour.

Whenever I hear people question whether God heals today (incredibly some still doubt this), I often think back to the simple testimony of that girl. "When I came to the meeting I was blind; and now I can see."

On one occasion I was listening to a minister give me all his reasons why God doesn't heal today, substantiating his arguments from Scripture, of course. There is usually little point in arguing; I simply asked him this question. "Do you expect me to say to a young woman who has just told me that when she came to the meeting she was blind and now she can see, that she must be mistaken because God doesn't heal today?" He gave me no answer.

I knew through this particular healing, the Lord was giving me some personal encouragement. I had been feeling pretty bad about my failure with the boy who had a tumour. When the disciples had asked Jesus why they had been unable to heal a boy, His response had been; "Because of your little faith!"

There are some diseases that I have found no difficulty in believing God to heal. I had known the healing of brain tumours before, but to me blindness seemed as great a physical healing as there could be. I had known several people to be healed who were partially sighted, or almost blind. Now the Lord was showing me the evidence of a totally blind person receiving sight through His healing power. That was a real encouragement and gave me an increase of faith for the future.

The lightning trip around South Africa ended at East London, where we stayed with Derek Crumpton, a man of vision and drive, who was mainly responsible for the national conference we had attended in Johannesburg. He was already receiving news of the tremendous working of God through the total ministry of that conference.

The whole of the three-week visit to South Africa had been a great faith-building time. Never had I seen the Holy Spirit move with such power, nor such a ready response among God's people. The experience confirmed my assessment that South

Africa was a most exciting country spiritually, for all its political problems.

The level of faith in Britain was somewhat different and one is always aware of the different spiritual climate when returning here. Yet the Lord is full of grace and often moves despite a lack of faith.

Soon after our return from South Africa, I was to speak one Saturday at renewal meetings in Bournemouth. About 700 were present, but the faithometer barely registered at the afternoon session. It was little better at the evening meeting. On such occasions it is tempting to adopt the attitude, "Let's not bother with any ministry today." That is not right; among the hundreds of people are those with great problems, whose faith has to be released and who need to see the evidence that God works in sovereign power. Even if it seems there is not much faith in the meeting, you can always follow obediently the leading of the Spirit, knowing that God is faithful to fulfil the promises of His word. This was just such an occasion.

To my amazement hundreds indicated that they were giving their lives to the Lord and had received the revelation that they now belonged to His Kingdom. And about 200 testified to being healed by the Lord. My comment to David: "That was a work of sheer grace on the Lord's part." That is always true when the Holy God touches the lives of His children; for truly we deserve nothing from Him.

There followed powerful times at Honiton, where a woman was healed of multiplesclerosis, Plymouth and Exeter. Then it was northwards to Manchester where we had one of the most powerful meetings I had experienced in this country. There must have been almost 2000 present in the Free Trade Hall and although numbers can only be approximate on such occasions, about 300 indicated that they had received the Lord for the first time and about the same number testified to healing.

After the meeting, there was a long line of people waiting to give brief testimonies about what God had done. Meanwhile

David and others were praying for folk who still needed ministry. The Lord was meeting with them and several came to join the queue to testify to the healing they had received.

One of those ministering was a man who had been converted in the local prison on my previous visit to Manchester. He had since been released and was a powerful witness for Jesus with a simple expectancy that He would work miraculously. God was certainly using him that evening.

I had been speaking about the lives God expects us to live as children of His Kingdom and quoted these verses: "Do you not know that the wicked will not inherit the kingdom of God? Do not be deceived; neither the sexually immoral nor idolaters nor adulterers nor male prostitutes nor homosexual offenders nor thieves nor the greedy nor drunkards nor slanderers nor swindlers will inherit the kingdom of God." (1 Cor. 6:9–10)

I sensed that God was calling people to repent of such things that evening, and after the service people representing every one of those things spoke with me, even a male prostitute. People are often locked in sinful ways, knowing that what they are doing is wrong, and yet lacking the incentive or the will-power to break free from that pattern of life. When confronted with their sin and need of repentance they are often relieved and grateful, even though the facing of their need may be difficult at first. If they respond, they are on the threshold of liberty and a new walk with Jesus.

One would expect non-Christians to be involved in such sin; however, many of the people concerned had made some kind of Christian commitment previously. It is possible to make a profession of faith in Jesus, or to conform to an externally religious life by attending church, while at the same time being in flagrant disobedience to the Word of God. Some never leave their former way of life and one can question the nature of their first commitment to the Lord. Others leave the sin of the past but allow the desire of the flesh to drag them back like a dog to its vomit.

In either case, our attitude is not to be one of judgment but of love, expressing the willingness of God to forgive and restore these children of His; to lead them to a deeper and more realistic relationship with the Lord Jesus: "If you hold to my teaching, you are really my disciples. Then you will know the truth, and the truth will set you free." (John 8:31–32)

11   Kingdom Faith

WE NEEDED A suitable title for our travelling ministry. We were concerned to extend the Kingdom of God, not promote the Bethany Fellowship. The Kingdom will only be extended effectively by faith in His Word, a faith that expects to see Him working mightily. "Kingdom Faith" seemed an appropriate name.

The symbol we chose represents the cost of our salvation as expressed in the crown of thorns, the victory of the cross over sin and death, and the sovereignty of the King of glory whom we serve.

In March 1980, David came with me on my third visit to Australia, an exciting prospect in view of all that had happened on my last visit. We spent four days in Brisbane, where the Lord began a significant healing in a woman who was set free from using the crutches she had needed for twenty years, having had polio as a child. She was overjoyed at being able to walk forward to receive Holy Communion for the first time, instead of having the bread and wine brought to her.

The time of ministry in Adelaide lived up to expectation; there was a great sense of anticipation after the events of my previous visit, and many hundreds flocked to the mission services. At a ladies' lunch thirty women gave their lives to the Lord, although I heard afterwards that one or two were upset that the gospel should have been preached on such an occasion! Many were also healed. I don't know if any objected to that.

In Canberra I ministered in Harry Westcott's church again. The church had really moved on since the mission there two years earlier. Their Sunday evening service was now held in a hotel ballroom, as the church building could no longer contain the numbers.

In Sydney there were notable times at an all-day seminar in the Town Hall and at Calvary Chapel, another congregation that had erected a new church since my previous visit because it had outgrown the old one. These signs of growth were truly encouraging.

There was a three-day ministers' conference at Calvary Chapel. The other speaker was a Pentecostal pastor from Brisbane who had seen his congregation grow from 70 to 1,500. He was now aiming for 4,000. Here was real vision and a genuine seeking of God to discover the principles of church growth. There is no doubt that big vision produces big results; small vision, small results.

The trip to Australia ended with visits to Hobart, Tasmania, Melbourne and a small country town called Kyabram. All the congregations of the town were led by Spirit-filled men and there was a keen sense of unity among them. A banner in the High Street announced our meeting; the mayor, who was a pentecostal lady, and the local bishop welcomed us; and hundreds packed into the conference hall. God answered the expectancy in the hearts of His people. When I asked people to stand if they wished to be baptised in the Holy Spirit, the bishop was first on His feet, followed by many others.

Once back in England we were quickly back on the road

ministering in places as varied as Chichester Cathedral, Trafal-
gar Square in London and the beautiful surroundings of
Ashburnham Place in Sussex. In June, Charles and I spent a
few days at the English-speaking church at The Hague and at
a healing conference that drew people from many different parts
of Holland.

Then it was off to the U.S.A. and Canada. Life was continuing
to be a whirl of meetings. Getting on a jet was more normal
than boarding a bus. However, this trip was to be different:
my wife, Caroline, was travelling with me. This was the first
time she had accompanied me on a ministry trip abroad. In the
past we felt it right that she should stay at home to care for
our children. I am away so often it seemed selfish to deprive
them of both parents simply because of our desire to be together.
We had never had peace in prayer that Caroline should come
with me until this trip. We would be away for only two weeks
and the children were well established in their new home and
schools.

We were crossing the Atlantic for three specific conferences.
The first was a regional conference of the Episcopal Charismatic
Fellowship at Akron, Ohio. This had a strong list of Anglican
speakers who had met together to prepare for a conference to
take place in Singapore during the following February.

The Canterbury Conference had given birth to SOMA (the
Sharing of Ministries Abroad). The concept was to promote an
exchange of ministries internationally, and specially to provide
Spirit-filled ministry for poorer countries where renewal had
hardly begun and which would be unable to invite speakers for
lack of finance. A shortage of money should not be allowed to
restrict the movement of renewal within the churches.

The speakers at this regional conference in Ohio included
members of the International Council of SOMA: The Archbishop of Cape Town, the Bishop of Singapore, Everett Fulham
and Charles Irish from the U.S.A., Cecil Kerr from Northern
Ireland and Michael Harper. A remarkable unity ran through
the main addresses even though there was no prior consultation
about its content, a true mark of the Holy Spirit's activity.

From Akron, Caroline and I flew to Ottawa for a brief mission that drew hundreds from around the city. Although I had visited Canada several times before, this was my first time of ministry in the capital.

From Ottawa we flew to Denver, Colorado, in a jet that seemed to land at just about every airfield en route. To crown everything we were caught in a violent storm and had to circle near Denver for an hour before it was safe to land. We were thrown around like a cork on the sea and it seemed that every joint in the jet creaked and groaned under the strain. It required all our concentration in prayer to keep our stomachs where they belonged.

After the flight, however, there was a beautiful drive to Snow Mountain Ranch, some 9,000 feet up in the Rockies. I was the guest speaker at the Diocese of Colorado Annual Renewal Conference, attended by about 1,350 people. The emphasis was on solid teaching of the Word and our place in Christ as members of His Body. On the Saturday evening there was a powerful time of ministry and about half those present indicated that they had received healing from the Lord.

On my trips abroad I was used to the love, care and concern which people extended to me. It was a great joy to see how much Caroline was appreciated. They obviously respected the vital part that she has to play in my ministry. More than that, they loved her as a person and we were greatly blessed by this time together.

It was also Caroline's first experience of how full and demanding these trips were. We had hardly any time to ourselves; the greatest problem was to find time to shop for some gifts to take home to the children.

What did all this travelling around to conferences and renewal meetings amount to? What was the fruit of it all? Is this really what God intended? Certainly God had been using such ministry. A great number of people had been brought to a personal relationship with Jesus Christ, or had been baptised in the Holy Spirit, or healed. There could be no doubting the personal blessings received. All those things had happened following the proclaiming of the Word of God, when important teaching could be given which, if put into practice, would lead people into a continuous growth in faith and loving obedience to the Lord. Jesus said: "Therefore everyone who hears these words of mine *and puts them into practice* is like a wise man who built his house on the rock." (Matt. 7:24)

The Lord had certainly used the network of regular renewal gatherings that were now taking place all over Britain. And yet there was a growing feeling in many places that these should stop because they had fulfilled their purpose. Renewal was not coming to an end but needed to enter another phase.

It was a great disappointment, for many others as well as myself, to recognise how slow churches were to face the issues involved in corporate renewal. Some ministers did not want to "rock the boat"; many congregations were content to persist in their traditional ways. Where there was positive leadership a work of the Spirit would grow and develop and praise be to God for the churches that have been moving on in His purpose in recent years! However, they are but a fraction of the whole number.

For many, corporate renewal was only spiritual theory. I was amazed at the number of situations where the minister was baptised in the Holy Spirit, but had not led the members of his congregation to personal experience of the Lord. I would sometimes ask a minister for an assessment of the spiritual state of the members of his congregation, what proportion knew the Lord, were filled with Spirit, were free in the use of spiritual gifts. Often I was met with a series of generalities, sometimes with an honest admission that he was unable to answer such questions. If the pastor does not know the spiritual condition of the members of his congregation, who is supposed to know? How does he know what to teach if he is ignorant of this basic information? Can he really have any vision of where he is leading the people?

Without such vision, it will be a matter of the blind leading the blind. The hundreds of people flocking to renewal rallies were the evidence that there were many who were not being pastored and fed properly in the churches to which they belonged. Every year I was seeing thousands commit their lives to Jesus for the first time. Yet many of them had been sitting in church pews Sunday by Sunday for years.

The great numbers coming to these meetings were also evidence of the new hunger that God was creating in the hearts of people when they met with Him in the power of the Holy Spirit—a hunger to be taught the Word of the Lord. It was plain that to bring somebody to new life in Jesus produced no guarantee that he would receive the teaching and encouragement necessary to enable him to grow in that new life. Renewal meetings provided some teaching, but not of the consistent nature that was required.

These rallies were a valuable opportunity for evangelism, but touched mainly those who were either within the structures of the denominational churches or were on the periphery of them. What about the masses of unchurched people beyond? Clearly this movement of the Holy Spirit had made no significant impression on the nation.

There was so much that needed to be done and to try to compress it all within a service lasting two or three hours was clearly inadequate; evangelism, teaching, repentance, praise, prayer, ministry in the Holy Spirit, healing. Properly, all these functions were the ministry of the local church.

Some ministers, who had been baptised in the Holy Spirit, had drifted back to their former ways of ministering largely in their own strength. They seemed disillusioned that renewal had not brought instant transformation to their congregations. Perhaps some reacted with fear to the opposition they encountered in facing people with their need of repentance and to be empowered with the Holy Spirit.

The signs of hope lay in the fact there were a considerable number of congregations who were wanting to move on with their ministers in obedience to the leading of the Holy Spirit. The rapid proliferation of new house churches was ample evidence that this was happening in only a few places. It may be true that some new groups consisted of proud, rebellious people who did not want to submit to the leadership in the churches where they belonged. But any such group quickly has troubles of its own, experiences division and passes into oblivion.

The house church movement cannot be written off in this way. Increasingly there have been frustrated and obedient Christians who have felt that God was calling them out of the denominations into new churches. They are not rebels, but those who have experienced their faith and spiritual life diminishing instead of growing because of the lack of sensitive, Spirit-filled ministry in the churches to which they previously belonged.

Any congregation manifesting the life and vitality of the Holy Spirit will not have the problem of people leaving with frustration because they are being led nowhere. The only ones who will want to leave such vibrant churches are those who are determined to go nowhere themselves.

God's anointing is clearly upon any group of people who are open to Him and willing to be faithful and obedient to Him, whether they be in the historic denominations or belong to a newly-formed fellowship. God will bless in either case and He will use all those who are open and willing to be used in His purposes.

Rallies and renewal meetings could do an ambulance job for many, keeping them alive spiritually while they remained loyal to their denomination upbringing; but this was hardly the ultimate purpose of God. People should be growing and maturing spiritually in the churches to which they belonged, not escaping from spiritual staleness for a breath of spiritual fresh air at a meeting. This was going to cause a crunch point at some time in the future.

In the seventies, God had been speaking prophetically to His Church, giving His people the opportunity to repent and to seek Him for the life and power that he makes readily available to His children. I, along with others involved in church renewal, had often urged people to remain in their churches as witnesses to others, to share the new life and vision God had given them, to love and serve as opportunity arose.

Now I sensed, again along with many others, that God's prophetic word was changing. Had the churches missed the opportunity that God had given them? If they persisted in their traditional ways, could they really be surprised if God bypassed them in what He wanted to do in the nation? Surely He would use all who were willing to be used in His purposes. But what if people were not willing?

The Kingdom teaching of the previous months impressed upon me where the heart of God lay. He wanted to see His Church built so that it could be effective and fruitful in taking the gospel of the Kingdom of God to the nation. I had a growing conviction that God wanted to meet powerfully with this nation; that the economic, political and social decline were all in the providence of God and would bring this country back to its knees.

To say that God wanted to meet with this nation meant that He was prepared to meet with this generation. Was He going to do that through the churches? Did He have to wait until the majority of denominational congregations were alive with the power of the Kingdom and spiritually equipped for effective evangelism? If so, at the present rate of progress, this generation would pass away to destruction long before finding the Lord Jesus Christ.

Were the new house churches God's answer to the dilemma? Only in part, just as the faithful denominational congregations would be used as a part of the answer. The Lord was going to mobilise all His forces, no matter what brand name they attached to themselves. What a need there was for His faithful people to work in unity, not in fear, mistrust, or in competition with each other.

It was encouraging to encounter increasingly the growing sense among discerning people that God was going to move in a mighty way in this land, a move of the Spirit that would transcend anything seen in recent years. Was this wishful thinking? I thought not. Would it happen out of the blue by God suddenly doing something dramatic? Certainly not. He plans carefully. He was preparing a people whom He could use to bring about a spiritual revival in this land. Evidence for that lay in the fact that an increasing number of people were receiving a burden from the Lord to pray faithfully for this nation. The rapid spread of the Lydia Fellowship in recent years is a significant indication of this. Intercessors for Britain and other such groups are all part of God's preparatory work. Before any time of spiritual revival, He gets His people praying, for it is on their knees that the victory for the spiritual future of Britain will be won.

If Jesus and the apostles needed to see the words of the gospel confirmed with signs and wonders, then we have that same need today. It would be sheer pride on our part, as modern Christians, to imagine that we could communicate the truth of Jesus Christ without the miraculous and supernatural elements of the gospel being expressed freely. Yet many churchgoing people are fearful of the supernatural power of God.

Neither were endless renewal services going to affect deeply the spiritual life of the nation, although they had been used in a significant way to bring many thousands of people into further dimensions of the Holy Spirit's activity. The gospel had to be expressed corporately in local fellowships; the cost of discipleship had to be seen in Christians' lives, both individually and corporately. There had to be an increased concern for the lost, expressed in both prayer and evangelism, at the local level.

For the past few years I had been responding to the stream of invitations to speak at conferences and renewal gatherings. We sensed that 1981 would be different, that we were not to go hopping around from one meeting to another. Instead we should concentrate on a series of short five-day missions, that would be evangelistic in emphasis.

The Lord began to speak clearly to us about the need of a systematic teaching course to be made available on cassettes. Groups could use such a course to prepare for a mission and new converts could be introduced into these groups. The material would also be ideal for the thousands of believers who were crying out for teaching.

There were several tape ministries which made conference and other teaching tapes available. These consisted mainly of long conference addresses which were not ideal for use in small groups or home fellowships. It is difficult to maintain concentration for more than twenty minutes when listening to a disembodied voice. Yet many such groups were hungry for teaching. All over the country I was hearing the same thing: "We have nobody to teach us." Often the local churches were not providing the teaching needed. In other cases, it was the ministers who were expressing a desperate need for consistent teaching to be given to the prayer or Bible-study groups within their congregations. They themselves did not feel they had an anointing from God to give the inspirational Bible teaching which they saw to be the need of their people.

All these comments served to reinforce what God was saying to us. There was a great need for a consistent course that would lead people through various stages of growth as disciples. It seemed right to begin a Kingdom Faith Teaching Course.

Each month a cassette would be made available, containing four twenty-minute talks, one for each week. These could be used privately but were intended primarily for use in small groups. Together with the cassette tape, work sheets would be made available. These would refer people to the relevant Scriptures, ask questions to draw out the substance of the teaching, and suggest ways in which the Word could be expressed in the daily lives of the listeners.

A few advertisements were placed in the Christian press in the summer of 1980 with a view to beginning the course in September. We believed that God was warning us that the response would be greater than we had expected. And so it proved to be. Over 600 groups immediately enrolled. That was evidence of both the hunger and the need. However, there was another purpose in beginning this Teaching Course. We saw it as a strategic part of our preparation for the Kingdom Faith Missions that were to take place during the following year.

Charles Sibthorpe and others began to prepare for the missions to be held in 1981 by introducing the Teaching Course to the participating churches about six months before the actual mission. Using the tapes and work sheets would be a good preparation but would also ensure that there were ample groups available into which it was possible to feed those who came newly to the Lord during the mission. It was irresponsible to bring people into the Kingdom and then leave them in a spiritual limbo. In some places they would be well cared for by the local churches, where they would be loved, encouraged, taught the Word of God and built up in their new-found faith. Unfortunately that was by no means universally true and it would be closing one's eyes to reality to believe that it was.

We have to make the necessary provision for teaching to be available — free, as part of our faith ministry. We were not out to make any profit, but to see the life of God's Kingdom extended. We would trust the Lord for financial provision.

The course begins with "The God of Grace", four talks about the gospel of salvation. This is followed by "The Gift of God", covering the ministry of the Holy Spirit. In subsequent months people are led on to understand the authority of the Word, the revelation of the Kingdom of God, how to live by faith and receive healing. There is teaching on our rich inheritance "in Christ Jesus", the Body of Christ, the renewal of the mind and the authority that we have in prayer.

Of the 600 groups that began in September, many belonged to denominational congregations, others were informal groups of hungry people and some had caught the vision that this course could be used evangelistically. They had begun a new group by simply inviting friends and neighbours to their homes.

Little purpose is served by waffle sessions, with people sitting back, cup of coffee in hand, airing their own opinions. Printed at the bottom of each work sheet is the reminder: "It is not my opinions that matter, Lord, but what you say in your Word".

There are now many thousands of groups throughout Britain and the rest of the world that are using this material. The course has been translated into several other languages and God is using it to encourage His people and build up His Body. When we respond to something that comes from the heart of God, He causes it to be fruitful for His own glory.

Throughout 1980 I was trying to find enough time to complete the writing of *In Christ Jesus*. The "in Christ" teaching was continuing to have a profound effect upon the life of the community and those who came among us for help. It met a great need when I taught publicly on the subject and it would be very helpful to put the teaching in book form. One could not hope to cover the vast sweep of this teaching in the New Testament in one or two talks.

I would be dealing with some of the most profound and difficult portions of Paul's epistles, and the teaching needed to be given in simple form that ordinary folk like myself readily understood. I was not one to write a theological treatise. It would be a book that would take people into the Scriptures so that they could discover for themselves the glorious revelation of the inheritance that God has given them as those who live in Christ.

The chief difficulty lay, not in placing deep truths in simple language, but in the spiritual opposition I encountered. It was clear that the adversary, the devil, did not want this book written. He did not want Christians to live in the power of their new natures; he spent all his time trying to encourage them to believe that they were still bound by the past, by sin and fear and a sense of personal inadequacy. He didn't want people to be directed to the truths of the Word of God that would set them free.

Every time I sat down to write I was aware of the oppressive attacks of the enemy, so much so that it was almost impossible to write on occasions. I would need to pray and take authority in the name of Jesus over the powers of darkness before I could make any headway.

Often I come across the attitude: "Oh, it's all right for you!" Some people imagine that characters like myself have "got it all together" and are immune from the pressures, problems and dilemmas that they encounter. Nobody has problems quite like their problems!

Anybody in Christian leadership will know that the pressures only increase as you move on in the purposes of God. Any ministry that proves fruitful for the Kingdom of God, Satan will do his utmost to destroy. But He who is in us is greater than he that is in the world. We have the victory in Jesus. However, we have to live in that victory and apply it in the daily circumstances of our lives. Time and again I have praised God for the way in which He has kept us from the spoiling work of the evil one; but we need to heed the warnings of Scripture and be vigilant against his devices.

The family came with me to the Scottish Churches Renewal Conference at St. Andrew's. That was a powerful conference with Jim Graham as the other guest speaker. When I spoke on the Sunday evening, I sensed that the Lord wanted to move powerfully among His people from the beginning of the conference. He wanted every one to know that He was present in His almighty power—and they were to believe Him to act accordingly. The first word of knowledge during the time of healing concerned someone suffering with a hernia. There was a shout of joy from one of the musicians who had been leading the worship.

He shared his testimony while clutching his trousers. Only a few days earlier he needed to have a surgical belt fitted because of the hernia. As soon as the word of knowledge was spoken everything moved back into place. "I felt it happen," he said with a mixture of joy and wonder. "The only trouble is the surgical belt slipped down and now my trousers are loose." That problem caused merriment but was easily remedied.

During the following days the lives of many were transformed as they were baptised in the Holy Spirit, and faith was encouraged by the further healings that took place. One man had been assigned to a wheelchair for the rest of his life, following an accident in which his spine was fractured. It was a common sight to see people lovingly carry him up the numerous steps of the University in his chair. By the middle of the conference, he was walking up them carrying his two young children in either arm. The healing had occurred during a time of prayer, when he was very aware of God's presence. The Lord told him to get out of his chair. It was impossible for him to stand because of his physical condition, but he obeyed and was immediately healed. No human ministry had taken place or was needed. Praise our wonderful God!

"Lord, I am not much of an evangelist; you will need to teach me." That was my prayer as we began the Kingdom Faith Missions in Cornwall in September. Evangelism had been part of my ministry; many had come into a personal relationship with Jesus Christ at meetings where I had spoken.

Even if the message is not directly evangelistic, a meeting that is under the direction of the Holy Spirit will be evangelistic because of the very fact that God is present and at work. In these missions the preaching was to be directed mainly towards those who were not, as yet, part of the Kingdom of God. I sensed that God wanted to teach me a new craft. I felt a complete novice and knew I needed to trust completely in Him.

Every sermon the Lord gave me was completely different; each occasion was a fresh adventure. As I spoke the Holy Spirit argued the truths of the gospel with clarity and purpose. Sometimes as the message unfolded, I couldn't understand the direction in which He was leading us. And yet, by the end, the Spirit had drawn all the loose ends together and had brought people to a place of repentance and commitment. I was as much a listener as others and rejoiced to hear from others that the Lord had spoken in a way that was particularly relevant to those present.

At Truro a number of people came to the Lord, including a middle-aged man with a military bearing. At the end of the service, he came to me, his face radiant. "I have been a good churchgoer all my life," he said. "Tonight I have met personally with Jesus." His appearance confirmed what he was saying. He explained that at various times he had heard others speak of the claims of Jesus Christ upon the lives of His people, but never in such a way that a response was demanded of him. That evening he had to make a response. Every subsequent evening that man sat near the front of the congregation wide-eyed with wonder as he soaked up the revelation of God's word.

There are many others like him. Part of them longs for reality, to meet the Lord Jesus personally; another part is fearful of doing so and of the cost that may be involved in allowing Him to exercise His lordship in their lives. What joy, relief and freedom when they do submit to Him!

The mission at Liskeard was to cover east Cornwall. Liskeard is a small town with only a few thousand inhabitants. It was good to stay in the same place for a few days; we could hear about what had been happening to people in a fuller way than was possible through the brief testimonies of healing that were customarily received.

In a place the size of Liskeard, the mission was the talk of the town. People were talking about it in the streets and the shops; those who had been were encouraging others to come.

As a result of the two weeks of ministry in Cornwall, several teaching groups were formed. We could be sure that everybody had material available to them to encourage their growth in faith and in knowledge of the Lord's love. We could not provide fellowship, but through the groups new Christians could be led into local churches.

The gospel that was proclaimed needed to be uncompromising in its claim upon people's lives. The level of repentance would determine the extent of the effectiveness and fruitfulness in each Christian's life. Many preachers have fallen into the trap of trying to make God acceptable to man. Quite the reverse is necessary; men need to be made acceptable to God, and He has provided the sacrifice of His Son on the Cross to make that possible.

If our heavenly Father causes heaven to rejoice over every repentant sinner, we too should rejoice. That we did. Besides those who came to the Lord many were baptised in the Spirit and healed as well. Many others came to a deeper assurance of their salvation and to a fresh repentance. If God is given the opportunity to work, He will work, no matter what the need.

Big crowds flocked to a four-day mission to Cheltenham, when the Lord moved in great power. A few weeks after our visit there, Don Double was ministering in the town. When it came to the time of healing he was amazed that only two or three people responded by asking for prayer. Usually in a large crowd there would be dozens, or hundreds even. He was perplexed and was quietly asking the Lord why more had not responded, when he suddenly remembered our visit.

Don asked all those who had received healing during our mission to raise their hands. A forest of arms were raised. Being the man he is, Don immediately gave glory to God for what He had done, a clear indication of the genuine healing that had taken place in many lives.

The leading of worship is an anointed ministry. It is not difficult to encourage people to sing spiritual songs, but that is not the same as leading people before the very throne of God in adoration and praise. When a meeting begins with worship in the Spirit, the Word will fall on more responsive hearts, already open to the Lord in praise and ready to receive His Word.

It is also a great advantage for a speaker to work with musicians that he knows, especially during the time of ministry when there needs to be a natural flow from prayer to praise, from repentance to rejoicing. The secret of leading worship is to minister to the Lord rather than the people. If the leader and musicians are centred upon the Lord in worship, they will soon gather the congregation with them into a similar place of praise.

Nothing is more frustrating than endless chorus singing. Worship should have direction and purpose, because the Holy Spirit has both.

Kevin Stares, who had joined the community with his wife Julie, was emerging as an anointed leader of worship. You tell an anointing by its fruit; to stand before hundred of people with a guitar and have them praising God and aware of His presence within a few minutes, demonstrates a true anointing. He and some of the other musicians from the community formed the basis of the mission team that went to Truro and Liskeard.

The community was growing steadily in size. In our corporate life we aim to encourage personal discipline, rather than impose it upon people. Neither do we remove the responsibility for decision-making from the individual and pass that over to the leadership. If the hearts of people are truly submitted to the Lord, there is no need for authoritarianism. That is only a fleshly substitute for genuine authority given by God. Where that genuine authority exists it is recognised and respected by others.

Our worship life is a joy. It is a great privilege to live among praising people whose deepest desire is to serve the Lord and be obedient to Him. I find it encouraging to come home from demanding times of ministry and relax in the worship life of the community. It was also a privilege to receive continual teaching of the Word and to be in a situation where that has been worked out in daily life.

The independence of ordinary church life enables a person to avoid many personal issues that cannot be avoided in community. Husbands and wives know how to work around each other's sensitive areas. In community you are living in close proximity to a number of people who may not share quite the same concern about your sensitive areas. That is to the good, for the Lord surely wants us to face up to those things, bring them to the Cross and see them healed. Community life should be a healing experience for all concerned.

It should also be a faith-building experience. We found that to be the case as we encouraged one another to confess positively the truth of who we are "in Christ Jesus". In the mornings we greet one another with the words: "It's another day of victory", to which the response is a very affirmative "amen". Every day is a day of victory if we believe the Scriptures. We are being led in Christ's triumphal procession, and each day should see victory over temptation, sin, fear, doubt, any nagging sense of inadequacy; victory of faith over feelings, victory of love in relationships.

Some people object to such talk. They say it is triumphal or unrealistic. Are Christians not supposed to be living in the victory of the Cross? Is it unrealistic to be living in the power of God's Holy Spirit and of His Word? He does not promise us immunity from opposition, difficulty, tribulation even; He does teach us to have faith to move mountains and urges us to have hearts and minds fixed on things above, where the victory has already been won, and not on circumstances or our negative reactions towards them.

Everything in the ministry was expanding rapidly. The numbers of the groups enrolling on the teaching course increased by about fifty per week. New equipment was needed. Our fast copiers were ideal for the travelling ministry but could not cope adequately with the growing demand. We were also in need of better equipment to improve the quality of the recordings. A high-quality sound reproduction system was needed for the missions. Nothing is more frustrating for people than not being able to hear distinctly at a meeting.

Such things cost plenty of money. As we laid the needs before the Lord, He provided. The money arrived, again without our making any appeals or asking people. Having acquired the equipment, we needed a suitable vehicle to transport it. It was also important to have a well-equipped bookstall available at each venue and adequately stocked with bibles and faith-building books. More money needed, more provision from the Lord, more thanks expressed to Him.

As the community grew, it obviously began to have more impact on the local area. Our main responsibility has always been to support those involved in the travelling ministries of evangelism and renewal. But more people from the locality were seeking help and ministry from us and those who remained at The Hyde were praying for the moving of the Holy Spirit in the churches of the district.

A small prayer meeting began with the local rector, two or three people from the village and a few from the community. This was never advertised, but the news soon spread and by the beginning of 1980 between forty and fifty people were coming regularly. Members of the community began to minister to several of these and had the joy of leading them to the Lord, to the power of His Spirit and into His healing grace. There was more than enough to do at home as well as on the travelling ministry. We needed more people — and the Lord promised to supply them.

We did not think it right to ask people to join us. As we travelled around, both David and I would receive the same witness independently of each other that certain people we met would become part of the community. If that was right, they had to hear the Lord for themselves. We were clear that everyone needed to know they had a personal call from God before they joined us. It would only be a question of time before we received a letter or telephone call saying: "It probably sounds ridiculous to you, but I cannot get rid of the idea that I should come and join the community."

Colin and Glennys Skeates and their children were the first from the local village of Handcross to join the community. Colin took charge of the tape ministry which was becoming an increasingly significant part of our work.

There were others who wanted to come and about whom we had no positive witness. Whoever approached us found that we did everything possible to show them that there was nothing glamorous in community life. It is a great privilege to be part of a group of people who live in an atmosphere of praise, love and faith. But the kind of life we live is uncompromising in its commitment: everything belongs to the Lord, all that we are and have.

Frequently while travelling we would be questioned about our community life. There was continual interest in how the finances were arranged, what happened to people's property, how the children coped with the change in lifestyle, and so on. Most of the time it was simple curiosity but on other occasions people were contemplating setting up communities of their own. If this was the case it was important to share some direct advice.

Community is not an end in itself. Any community needs to have a reason for its existence. It must be for the glory of God, but also it should have some particular ministry to the wider Body of Christ or the world. The Lord does not bring people to live together for the sake of it, but because He wants their lives to be more fruitful.

As the community grew it became more ecumenical, with new folk coming from a variety of church backgrounds. We have never insisted that everyone adheres to any system of doctrine; but it is clear that we seek to see the Word of God lived out in our lives. Jesus promises that the Holy Spirit will guide us into all truth, not that any of us possesses the perfect knowledge and understanding of truth already. We respect each other's differences without ever allowing them to divide us. The life we live in the power of the Holy Spirit transcends any differences.

If we are to see the unity that is the aspiration of many Christians, we will need to realise that this will not happen by simply talking and praying while we hold on rigorously to our denominational stances. Those denominational attitudes have to go to the Cross so that we can begin to learn from one another and can see the Holy Spirit joining our lives in love and worship. Coming together for ecumenical services will never achieve unity; neither will conferences by church leaders and theologians.

True unity will be seen only where Christians are prepared to emerge from their denominational ghettos and begin to share their lives as one. Such groups will be a prophetic witness to the churches. It seemed clear that we, as a community, were to be such a witness.

The weekly meetings at the Hyde continued growing and attracted up to 150 people every week, the limit we could accommodate. What had begun as a prayer group with two or three visitors had expanded without any publicity, but simply through the personal witness of those whose lives were touched by God at the meetings. From the start we had resolved that such a meeting should not revolve around my personal ministry. It needed to centre upon the Lord and the working of His Holy Spirit through the community.

On the few occasions I was present, it was a strange feeling to wander unrecognised among so many people in my own home. "Are you one of the community?" I was asked on one occasion.

"Who is Colin Urquhart?" someone was overheard saying on another. Such things caused me to rejoice. That is just as it should be; the work growing because of the evident ministry of the Holy Spirit and not through the reputation of any man.

David played the key role of the teacher and led most of the times of ministry. God's anointing upon him was apparent to all. I had to face a painful decision.

For eighteen months David had been a constant travelling companion. I had grown to love and value him deeply in the Lord. He was a great encouragement to me and it had been really important to be able to agree with him in prayer. However, I was not to hold on to him. A pastor for the community at The Hyde was needed to build the lives of those who were joining us. A teacher was needed for the meetings there. Someone had to oversee the ministry to those who came seeking counsel and healing. David had received plenty of concentrated experience in the time he had been travelling with me and it was impossible to avoid what the Lord was saying; David was the one who must remain at home to fulfil these roles. His place would not be taken by an individual but by the team that would be involved with me on the Kingdom Faith Missions.

He had already moved with his family out of the main building into a house in the village. We had exhausted the buildings available on the estate and the future growth of the community would need to take place there.

As David began to grow in the new responsibilities that God had given him, I could only praise Him for all that He had done in the life of this dear brother.

Yes, 1981 was going to be different, but it was going to be great. We were serving the great Lord and King. What we didn't realise was that it would be the year when the totally unexpected was to happen.

"JUST LIKE PENTECOST!" That was how some pastors described the last meeting of a clergy conference for the diocese of Gothenberg. The bishop and seventy of his clergy had come to a retreat centre on the west coast of Sweden, run by Bengt Pleijel, a dear man of God who now distributes the Kingdom Faith Teaching course in Swedish.

Externally the temperature was very cold; the sea was frozen for several hundred yards. However, the Lord warmed the hearts of His children and nearly everyone at the conference asked for personal ministry to be baptised in the Holy Spirit.

Caroline and I then travelled to Stockholm for a national conference held in the Katerina Church. Before going to Sweden I had been warned by others with experience of ministry there not to be put off by the apparent lack of response among the people. I soon discovered what they meant. At the opening session, the Lord gave me a powerful prophetic word to share with the conference. The people sat in the vast church building with expressionless faces. Were they really receiving what was being said? The translation sounded good and the interpreter was preaching along with me under an obvious anointing.

After the session, one person after another told me how the Lord had ministered to them through the address. Many were astonished that it spoke so clearly and directly to the national scene in Sweden although I had no personal knowledge of that. "This must be published," was the verdict of the leadership of the conference; "it is more than a message for the people here. It is a message from God to the whole church in Sweden."

It was published, together with other prophetic addresses by speakers at that conference. In Sweden I was assured that these would be widely read by church leaders and received by them.

Repentance was the key theme of the conference. The Lord's people must demonstrate the life of His Kingdom and unity with one another within this Body of Christ so that the world could see an alternative to the society that is crumbling around them. Leaders need to face the cost of obedience to the Lord in what He is asking of them in leading His people in the way of the Spirit. By the end of the conference the joy of the Lord had broken through the dour appearance of the assembly as a Spirit of praise came upon the people.

There was one particularly powerful address given by a Danish pastor who pointed out the sin of talking and thinking about ourselves in denominational terms. Every time we do so we sin, it was said, for we perpetuate the division and disunity that is an offence to God, who desires to see His Body one.

This came with the authority of a clear word from God and brought great conviction to the gathering. I could identify with so much of what was said and the difficulty of breaking out of denominational thinking.

When leaving Luton I little realised how deeply I was still affected by denominational attitudes. I had been concerned to see a more realistic unity between Christians from different traditions and backgrounds. Every Sunday evening service at St. Hugh's was a unity service in the Spirit. There would be Roman Catholic nuns, Salvation Army officers, members of Brethren Assemblies all mixed together with Baptists, Methodists, Pentecostals and those from the reformed traditions. Neither had our Anglicanism ever prevented us from being obedient to the Lord in following His Spirit.

As I began to travel and minister more freely across the denominational spectrum I realised how little I knew and under-stood of the way that other Christians thought. Since then I have been learning greatly from those of different persuasions.

There is much to be gained from holding together the particular insights that are cherished by different groups.

It has disturbed me greatly to hear so many ministers affirm that they cannot be obedient to what they know the Lord is saying to them and their congregations "because of the denomination". There can never be any excuse for disobedience to the Lord. He is ready to meet people where they are and to move among any fellowship where people will be open to His Spirit and His purposes, regardless of any denominational or non-denominational tag. But the blessing stops as soon as any group is disobedient and begins to resist the Lord's purposes.

What is the purpose of singing our hymns and songs of praise to the Lord, if at the same time we are being wilfully disobedient to Him? No excuse will suffice. He knows the circumstances and pressures better than we do. He would not lead people in a particular way unless He wanted them to obey, regardless of the cost.

Although He will work within historic structures, God will not be confined to them; neither will He allow His Holy Spirit to be restricted by the limitations men place upon Him. For any Christian group to place limits on the working of God through His Spirit is simply to invite Him to work elsewhere. And that He will surely do, wherever people are ready to face the cost of being obedient to Him.

Many seem to lack any vision beyond the renewal of a denominational congregation, and even that is often limited to a desire for a little more love, praise and commitment without disturbing those who do not want to be disturbed. Often the Holy Spirit disturbs us before He comforts. In His Word, the Lord says that He will wound and heal. Obedience can only result from the Lord facing us with our disobedience and desire to compromise His Word and purposes.

Denominational thinking can be so deeply rooted that a person may not readily recognise it within himself. It is even suggested by some that disloyalty to the denominational tradition is disloyalty to God himself. But He is not made in the image of any denomination.

May we be open to learn from one another, while exercising true discernment of the Spirit. When we enjoy the glory of heaven we will all discover we have been wrong; none of us has the perfect understanding and grasp of the truth. Let us pray, therefore, that the Lord will deliver us from bias and prejudice and attitudes that limit the working of His Spirit in our lives and ministries. He desires to see His Church built, not denominational intransigence perpetuated.

From Stockholm, Caroline and I travelled westwards to Skova by train. We received several warm looks and smiles from passengers who had been to the conference, and one young man invited us for coffee in the buffet car where he introduced us to other friends. They were full of what the Lord had been doing among them during the last few days. We went with them to their carriage for prayer. What better way to use the journey; it was not going to be the rest I had anticipated.

We prayed and rejoiced together, joining hands as we sang "We are one in the Spirit" in a mixture of Swedish and English, much to the astonishment of the ticket collector. He was not used to such sights on his train.

As preparations for the missions were being made I was faced by a number of salutary truths. Ministers and leaders had not objected to characters like myself speaking at renewal gatherings in their towns. There was no obligation for them to attend and if they wanted to discourage their people from coming, they were in a position to do so.

But to set foot in an area with evangelistic intent proved to be a very different matter. Some incredible reactions came bubbling to the surface. I can fully respect that there are different concepts and methods of evangelism, but it was difficult to avoid the impression that some had no intention of bringing the gospel to the lost and didn't want anybody else to do so either. For others the main concern was: "Who is going to have the new converts? How are they going to be introduced to the churches?" Somehow the concern for the people seemed to be only secondary.

As a result most of our missions were officially supported by some churches and boycotted by others. That did not mean that the people stayed away. During one mission I was told of a certain minister who was telephoning members of his congregation, telling them definitely not to come to the meetings. I am not sure of the cause of his objections or whether he only succeeded in stimulating the interest of his congregation. Anyway, by the end of the mission several had come and, I understand, been baptised in the Holy Spirit and received healing.

Our first mission in 1981 was held at Salisbury. At one of the meetings a daughter stood up and believed in the Lord to heal her mother from angina and hiatus hernia, from which she had suffered for many years. For a long time she had been taking strong pain-killing drugs. Two nights later the mother herself told how she was now healed and able to do things she had not done for years. She also related with much joy how the Lord had healed her of multiple sclerosis twenty-seven years previously.

It was also at Salisbury that we met Iolo (pronounced "Yollo"), a burly fisherman from Barmouth in North Wales. During the previous October, he was on a fishing trip in the Hebrides and put into port at Stornaway. He visited the Seamen's Mission where he was played a tape from the Kingdom Faith Teaching Course on the power of the Holy Spirit. In response, he gave his life to Jesus and asked to be filled with the Spirit.

Iolo's wife, Gloria, was at home in Wales awaiting surgery for internal problems and suffering from back trouble. Iolo telephoned her with news of the transformation God had brought about in his life and said he knew God could heal her.

It was some weeks before he returned home and a prayer meeting could be arranged. He had asked the Lord to lead him to some folk who would be able to pray with them and minister the Lord's healing to Gloria. However, while at home he received the news that during a storm his boat had sunk in Portree Harbour.

The temptation was to go rushing back to Scotland to recover his boat. But what about Gloria? When he prayed, he sensed that the Lord was telling him to put the prayer before the boat. He obeyed. As they prayed the pain went and later the healing was complete and the hospital appointment cancelled. Iolo returned to Portree and the boat was refloated. Without serious delay he was back at sea.

Iolo came forward in response to a word of knowledge about the healing of his eyes at the first meeting at the mission, and told me his story. Salisbury is a long way from Barmouth, further still from Scotland. Amazingly, Iolo had never been to a service where he had known the power of the Holy Spirit to be at work. He had tried churches around his home, but what he had heard on that tape was not happening there — and he wanted reality. After all, he knew that something real had happened to him and his wife.

He had decided to drive to Salisbury in his van. He had enrolled on the tape course and received our newsletter. He would go in search of what he had heard about. That evening was a revelation to him and he delayed his return home so that he could attend further meetings. He gave his testimony at one of these to the glory of our great and wonderful God.

We were receiving great encouragement from the initial response to the Kingdom Faith Teaching Course. It was filling a great need and God was using it not only to teach, but to draw people to experience His power in their lives in different ways. Our tape office was receiving a constant stream of letters testifying to His gracious working. The groups themselves varied greatly. Some were large, church-based groups; others of a more informal nature.

Ours is the smallest possible group, just myself and my wife who have been churchgoers all our lives. I think we have learned more about true Christianity from your first six lessons than in the last forty years.

Another correspondent wrote:

The members' ages range from seventy-eight to ninety-four and there are five of us. I am the youngest at seventy-eight, and was responsible for starting the group which meets every week for worship, sharing and study of the Word.

Who said that people could be too old to be renewed? At the other end of the scale some schools were using the tapes for their meetings. Sometimes letters testified to personal blessing:

He released me from the bondage of Satan that had chained me down for so long and as a result I experienced a wonderful freedom of worship. I really pray now that I will be able to go on and live the faith that I have been given through the power of the Holy Spirit. I really want to work for God and do His will. He has done so much for me! I want to continue to live in the strength of His Spirit so that I can continue Christ's work to the glory of God.

Another wrote:

You really have been blessed of the Lord and through your tape ministry I have come to know the Lord in a way I never thought possible. The series has blessed me tremendously — I cannot begin to thank you.

And there were many testimonies of healing:

This tape in particular has spoken very powerfully to us, and we do thank the Lord for the Word that He gave you. We are currently rejoicing in the gracious healing of one with shingles when the sight of one eye was endangered. He has graciously restored the sight and rapidly healed the condition.

I quote these letters from the current edition of *Kingdom Faith News*, a printed newsheet that has replaced our duplicated prayer letter. Our printing department was becoming a full-scale operation. Don Skinner, together with his wife, Joan, had joined us with a long experience of graphics and the printing trade. He was now responsible for this part of the Kingdom Faith ministry.

The rapid spread of the Teaching Course led to a need to become computerised. We laid the need of a computer before the Lord and a few days later received a telephone call from someone who said that he had ordered a computer for us and was posting a cheque to enable us to pay for it when it arrived. We praised the Lord for His graciousness and the faithful generosity of the one through whom it had been provided.

Soon after the Salisbury mission I went to Singapore for the world-wide Anglican leaders conference, organised by SOMA. I travelled with Michael Barling, who was then director of the Fountain Trust and was to join us at The Hyde later in the year.

During the conference I spoke at an evangelistic service in the cathedral. The building was packed, with others standing outside. As is the custom there, those who had never been to a Christian meeting before were asked to raise a hand. Several arms were raised.

While the opening time of praise was taking place, the Lord prompted me to turn to Isaiah 40. The opening verses of that chapter hold a special place in my heart, for they were the first verses of Scripture that ever came alive for me when I was a young lad: "Comfort, comfort my people, says your God." The words had been a personal call and commission from God. Did the Lord want me to speak on these opening verses?

No, the Spirit showed me that I was to read the whole chapter. It is fairly long and I wondered what purpose God could have. Usually people can only concentrate on the reading of a few verses at a time. Still, there is no point in arguing with the Lord.

I had never experienced such an anointing in the reading of Scripture before. The message of that whole chapter was so relevant for an evangelistic service in a place like Singapore, where there is much idol-worship: "To whom, then, will you compare God? What image will you compare him to?" By comparison to Him, men are as grasshoppers and the nations as "dust on the scales". The chapter goes on to declare sovereignty of God the Creator. Were we all prepared to bow to the sovereignty of God in our lives? Were the non-Christians prepared to bow the knee to Jesus as Lord? Were the Christians prepared to acknowledge the supremacy of Jesus in every area of their lives?

After a prayer of repentance, I asked the entire congregation to stand. I invited them to literally bow their knees to Jesus, but only do so if this was an act that came from the heart. Every person in that cathedral knelt before the sovereign Lord Jesus Christ. There was an awe-inspiring silence upon the gathering. People were meeting personally with Jesus.

I asked those who had never submitted their lives to Jesus before to come forward. Counsellors were ready to minister to them but in the event could not cope as people streamed forward filling every inch of room at the front. It was an awesome experience to be surrounded by so many people meeting with the Lord.

The vision of SOMA was to take ministry to areas of the world where renewal was needed but where speakers would not normally be invited. From Singapore the 150 delegates were to spread out to India, and across South-East Asia. I had been asked to go to Kuching, the principal city of Sarawak.

My visit there had only been arranged a few weeks before. When I arrived I discovered that the Anglican congregation of the church where the mission took place was a very large one, but few were baptised in the Holy Spirit. I was told that relatively few had a personal relationship with Jesus or any assurance of their salvation. Many worshipped in church on Sunday but were still steeped in the superstitious practices of their forefathers and would be more likely to consult the witch-doctor than the priest, if sick.

Within this large congregation was a group of young people, one of whom had met with the Lord while at college on the mainland and had been baptised in the Spirit. On his return to Kuching a group of about twenty young people responded to this young man's bold witnessing for the Lord. In that society the old do not listen to the young, and it seemed that nobody else was concerned to experience the power of the Spirit in their lives.

The group began to pray that the Lord would send someone to proclaim the gospel clearly to the people, someone to whom they would listen. They saw my visit as a direct answer to that prayer and organised among themselves a chain of prayer throughout every day until the mission. When the ground has been prepared by prayer you know the Lord is going to work. Literally hundreds came to the Lord during that mission. Many were healed and filled with the Spirit.

A woman who spoke only Chinese was brought by friends. Although there was no translation she understood every word I said; the Holy Spirit was obviously translating for her. God was working in miraculous ways.

I was taken by the archdeacon, who was vicar of that church, on a visit to a "Christian village" in the jungle. This was my first experience of a longhouse village and very interesting it was. When we arrived I was greeted by a man as I was climbing out of the Land Rover. Underneath each arm he carried a live chicken. "This your dinner," he said. And it was, cooked on the ground outside the simple building that served as a church hall.

I was warmly received by the local parish priest and some of the church council. "I Anglican, I Anglican," was the boast of many I met.

"Lord, forgive us," I was praying on the way back to Kuching. "What have we done? Please, Lord, forgive us."

At great personal cost, missionaries had taken our dear Anglican tradition and planted it in the middle of the jungle. There were all the trappings but none of the reality of the living Jesus. I wanted to stay and tell them the good news, but I had to return to the city, where I was asked about my reactions to my visit to the village. When I shared honestly what I had felt, others nodded their heads in agreement. "And it is sad that the others have done it too," I was told. "We could take you to a Roman Catholic village, or a Methodist village, or a Baptist village and you would find much the same thing."

The sin and pride of our denomination divisions! Fortunately, I was assured, there were also villages where the Spirit of God was moving powerfully and the bishop told me that he had requests from villages deep in the jungle to send evangelists. They had heard a gospel message on the radio and wanted to know more! He had nobody to send! How many great opportunities there are to see the Kingdom of God spread on earth! "Whom shall I send? Who will go for me?"

It was such a blessing, after that experience, to see hundreds come to the Lord that evening.

13   To Be Like Jesus

IT SEEMED SUCH a simple prayer. "Lord, give us your faith for this mission." But what dynamic consequences it was to have for us!

To advertise the details of the meetings, Bible markers had been prepared for each of the Kingdom Faith missions. At the bottom of these slips of card this brief prayer had been printed. It seemed appropriate. We wanted the Lord to be glorified in each of the missions. We wanted to see them with the eyes of His faith, so that His purpose for them could be fulfilled.

The mission to Southport, in Lancashire, was about to begin and I was preparing for the opening meeting. "Don't be surprised if I answer that prayer," the Lord said. At first I could not understand what He meant. Then He explained: "My faith for these missions is that you leave revival behind you. But you do not have that faith."

He was absolutely right. I was expecting the Lord to bring many people into His Kingdom, to fill them with the Holy Spirit and to perform signs and wonders. I had seen touches of revival when ministering in other countries, but I had not expected such a challenge to my faith as this.

I could hardly encourage others to have God's faith for the mission if I did not have it myself. I was due to meet for prayer with the rest of the team and shared with them what I believed God had said. None of us had even thought of expecting revival and we had to confess our unbelief to the Lord and ask Him to give us the faith that we lacked.

We prayed more during that mission than in any previous time of ministry and we saw fruit as a result. As our ministry came out of our life together in the community, we needed to share with the rest what God was showing us. "You can only give to others what you have yourselves. You can take revival to other places if you are yourselves revived."

What did God mean by this? We had experienced the renewal of our lives by the power of the Holy Spirit. So what was He asking of us now? Although we saw blessing in that Southport mission we were not aware of leaving revival behind. We had some seeking of the Lord to do.

As I shared these things with the leaders of the community, we took down from our shelves books about revival that we had read in past years. Charles Finney's little book *Finney on Revival* [E. E. Shelhamer (ed.) Dimension Books, Bethany Fellowship Inc., Minnepolis] was of particular value. There he maintained that revival could happen in any place at any time, so long as God's people were prepared to pay the cost. He said that most people thought of revival as a sovereign move of God that comes unexpectedly. God does not work on impulse; He plans carefully and prepares the hearts of His people. The only reason why His children do not see revival in the nation is that their own hearts are not right before God. When they are right with Him and with one another, then those sovereign moves of God will be seen. They are not the revival itself, but the fruit and the result of the revival that takes place among God's own people.

Finney had a long experience of revival and he should know what he is talking about. We had some heart-searching to do.

What happens in a time of revival? Sinners come readily under the conviction of the Holy Spirit; they are so burdened by a sense of sin that they turn to the Saviour Jesus. They have such a vital experience of the forgiveness of God that they are immediate witnesses to those who are still bound by sin. Did we really have that effect upon people who came among us? They received blessing and healing and we led many to repentance and new life; but somehow we knew that God was speaking of another dimension of His life that we were not manifesting freely.

What was wrong in our hearts? Finney suggests that there are a number of factors which prevent revival: wrong relationships and attitudes towards others, dissension with those in authority, jealousy, speaking evil of others, worldliness, secret sins, laxity in spiritual discipline, unreliability, hardness of heart (especially towards God's Word), unholiness, a lack of openness towards others.

There can be many things lacking in the lives of Christians which hinder revival in their own hearts and the lives of others around them; a lack of gratitude and love towards God; neglect of the Bible, prayer, family duties, watchfulness over oneself and one's brethren; neglect of self-denial and the means of grace. God's purposes are further hindered by unbelief, worldly-mindedness, pride, envy, slander, censoriousness, levity, lying, cheating, hypocrisy, robbing God, bad temper and hindering others from being useful.

When confronted with such a list of sins we could well understand why we had not experienced revival. As we searched our hearts concerning each of these things we were readily drawn to repentance by the Lord. There were so many wrong attitudes and motives that He needed to correct in us.

In recent weeks the Lord had shown us that our minds needed to be renewed. They were a battlefield; we had thoughts we did not want and that were dishonouring to the Lord: unholy thoughts, impure thoughts, proud thoughts, selfish thoughts, wandering thoughts when praying, and so on. The mind is the first line of attack for the enemy. If he can disrupt our thinking, he will succeed in robbing us of peace and will sow confusion and anxiety instead. And our thinking determines our actions; wrong thinking will produce wrong actions.

God intends each of His children to be in full control of his thinking, every thought taken captive for Christ. Our minds were not to be the plaything of the enemy. We were to exercise our spiritual authority over the powers of darkness, so that they could not influence our thinking or disrupt the work of the Spirit in our lives: "The weapons we fight with are not the weapons of the world. On the contrary, they have divine power to demolish strongholds. We demolish arguments and every pretension that sets itself up against the knowledge of God, and we take captive every thought to make it obedient to Christ." (2 Cor. 10:4–7)

Paul teaches that the god of this age has blinded the minds of unbelievers; but we were believers who had received the light of Christ. Every area of darkness needed to be confronted and dismissed from our minds. We asked the Lord to show us any stronghold the enemy might have in our thinking. Some were obvious, others hidden except to the gaze of the Holy Spirit. As the Lord revealed these, we came against them in the name of Jesus.

It had been disheartening to realise how easily Satan had access to our minds. As we used the shield of faith to parry the flaming darts of the evil one and reject these negative, critical, impure and unholy thoughts we discovered the truth of the Scripture afresh: "Resist the devil and he will flee from you."

He was not to have any strongholds in our thinking. If he had, that was only because our hearts were not right with God or with others, and the enemy was able to capitalise on that area of sin. If our hearts were not right, then neither would our thinking be right, nor our speech, our relationships nor our actions. We had to deal with the negative; we needed also to seek God for the positive work that He wanted to do within us.

Members of the community had been free to disperse with their natural families over Easter. It was suggested we should all ask the Holy Spirit to convict us of any wrong motive, intention or attitude of the heart, and bring us to a new depth of repentance. We had to keep our eyes on Him and our ears attentive to what He was saying to each of us. We were not indulging in some inward-looking, introspective time of self-examination. We wanted the Lord to show us our hearts as He saw them.

What He showed us, none of us liked. We were indeed moved

to a new depth of heartfelt repentance. I think everybody was amazed at how many wrong motives, intentions and desires they had.

As we gathered again after the holiday, it was apparent that many had already met with the Lord in significant ways. Repentance always leads to a fresh release of the Spirit's activity in a person's life. But some of us were far from satisfied.

Even though the Lord had been meeting with individuals as they allowed Him to search their hearts and draw them to a new repentance; and even though we were experiencing much victory in our thinking as a result of the renewal of the mind teaching, still something was missing. God wanted and needed to *do* something specific among us. What was the missing dimension that would lead to this revival of which He had been speaking? That was the question that I put to the Lord; and He showed me the answer.

In the past few years His children had been seeking Him for several different dimensions of the life of His Spirit. They had sought Him for His love, His power, His joy and peace; they had sought Him for healing and for gifts; they had asked for the fruit of the Spirit in their lives.

"But you do not believe in the Father, Son and loving Spirit, even though He is love. And you do not believe in the Father, Son and joyful Spirit, although He gives joy. Neither do you believe in the Father, Son and peaceful Spirit, or healing Spirit, or powerful Spirit, although all those are aspects of His work.

"You believe in the Father, Son and *Holy* Spirit, because it is my essential nature to be *holy*."

People were prepared to seek those dimensions of the life of the Spirit that they wanted, but *who wants to be holy*? Were we prepared to seek Him to make us holy, even as He is holy?

What does it mean to be holy? Put simply, it means we are to be like Jesus. One Scripture after another revealed this to be His expectation for His children:

For he chose us in him before the creation of the world to be holy and blameless in his sight. (Eph. 1:4)

And to put on the new self, created to be like God in true righteousness and holiness. (Eph. 4:24)

But now he has reconciled you by Christ's physical body through death to present you holy in his sight, without blemish and free from accusation — if you continue in your faith, established and firm, not moved from the hope held out in the gospel. (Col. 1:22–23)

God disciplines us for our good, that we may share in his holiness. (Heb. 12:10)

Make every effort to live in peace with all men and to be holy; without holiness no one will see the Lord. (Heb. 12:14)

But just as he who called you is holy, so be holy in all you do; for it is written: "Be holy, because I am holy." (1 Pet. 1:15, 16)

"Holy" means literally "set apart" for God. He desires a holy people, those whose lives are set apart for Him; to be used for Him, but above all to be like Him. Man has been made in His image. Sin has marred that image; but God has undone the work of sin on the cross. The precious blood of Jesus cleanses us from sin, from what prevents us reflecting His image and glory in our lives.

God has given us His *Holy* Spirit to live within us, to form Jesus in us. The Spirit is to flow out of our innermost being as rivers of living water so that He might be revealed to the world through our humanity.

"Do you want to be like Jesus?" That seemed to be the simple question He was asking us.

Our initial response was "Yes, of course we want to be like Him." In which case, the Lord showed us, everything in our lives that was not like Him would have to go. Were we prepared for that? Some of us hesitated. We wanted to be like Jesus and to express His life more perfectly; but there were things about ourselves that we didn't want changed, self-righteous attitudes and our selfish preferences, for example.

However, the Lord had prepared the ground well for what

He was saying to us now. The previous weeks of repentance had led to a deeper work of the cross in our lives. It was not good enough to come to the Lord again and again confessing the same sins and asking for His forgiveness. We needed to do that; it was right to do that; and He would always forgive because He had promised to do so: "If we claim to be without sin, we deceive ourselves and the truth is not in us. If we confess our sins, he is faithful and just and will forgive us our sins and purify us from all unrighteousness." (1 John 1:8–9)

And yet there needed to come a cry from our hearts: "Lord, change me so that I do not persist in the same sins. Lord, break me of the desire to sin. Give me your hatred of sin so that I draw back from it."

Has not the Lord promised to grant us the desires of our hearts? Yes, that was where the problem lay: our hearts needed to be revived. We needed to have the same desires and attitudes as Jesus. "Your attitude should be the same as that of Christ Jesus: Who, being in very nature God, did not consider equality with God something to be grasped but made himself nothing, taking the very nature of a servant." (Phil. 2:5–7)

We needed to humble ourselves before the Lord, to realise our nothingness before Him. The impress of the cross had to become more evident in our lives. Humble yourselves, therefore, under God's mighty hand, that He may lift you up in due time." (1 Pet. 5:6)

I had come to the point at which I needed a new breakthrough with the Lord — and so did everyone else in the community. The repentance of the past few weeks had been fruitful, but it was incomplete. Somehow we needed to meet with God in His holiness. Was such a thing possible? How could it happen?

It was Friday, May 1st, 1981. The members of the mission team were praying together. Ahead lay the spring holiday weekend, a time when we could be with our families before the busy summer of travelling for the missions. On the following Tuesday we would be off on a whirlwind tour of meetings to prepare for these missions.

Suddenly there came the realisation that whatever this revival was that needed to happen to us, it hadn't happened. We still did not have the Lord's faith for these missions.

I was crying out in my heart to God. "What do we have to do, Lord?" I felt a great agony in my soul. He answered my prayer: "Abandon all your plans for the weekend and seek me." I shared that with the others and the reaction of some was plain. For us, a long weekend with our families was a luxury. But the Lord made it clear that if we were not prepared to face the cost of such a sacrifice we could forget the rest. What had Charles Finney said about the cost of revival?

The news soon spread throughout the community. Saturday would be a day of prayer and all the adults would meet together at seven p.m.

On that Saturday I sensed a longing in some to meet with the Lord. That was certainly the desire in my heart. In others there was a reticence, a fear perhaps. As the day progressed people were moved by the Spirit to confess their negative responses and seek the Lord's forgiveness.

Saturday, May 2nd, seven p.m. The community meets together, packed into the library at The Hyde. The praise and singing begins. Silence falls upon the gathering. A few confess their negative reactions at having to spend the holiday seeking the Lord; others express their longing to meet with Him.

A simple prayer is forming in my heart: "Lord, please come and meet with us in your holiness." Inwardly I begin to pray those words over and over again, begging the Lord to respond to them. I speak the same prayer out loud and it is echoed by several others. The Holy Spirit has created the same desire in their hearts.

There is a word of prophecy. God speaks to the hearts of His children and suddenly it seems that Jesus walks into the room, the Holy Jesus. Immediately people start falling to their knees. Next they are lying prostrate, on their faces before the

Lord. One person after another is crying out to the Lord for His mercy. Open confession of sin is happening, one person after another. The secrets of hearts are being revealed. The presence of others doesn't matter; nothing can remain hidden in the Holy Presence of Jesus. There is only a longing to be right with the risen Saviour.

There are many tears, much beseeching of the Lord in tongues, many praying aloud at once. An hour, two hours and still people are prostrate before the Lord. Many have come to a place of peace; more than that, they are clean. "Create in me a clean heart, O God, and renew a right spirit within me," King David had prayed.

The Lord had come among us and revealed His holiness. In those brief hours the Lord had shown more to us about our hearts than all our weeks of searching had revealed. We all felt as if we had been through the mill — and some of us were definitely not out of it yet. We needed to go on seeking the Lord. There could be no holding back now, no turning back either. More was at stake than our own personal lives; God was calling us to take revival to others. What He was doing among us now must bear fruit for His glory.

Sunday morning, and the community meets for worship. Holy Communion is somehow more holy than before, and there is something different about the worship, a new depth, a sense of adoration, a touch of gentleness and graciousness that was not there before.

Sunday evening, and all the adults meet together again in the library. What will happen? Will it be like the previous evening? Was that a once-only experience?

Our questions are soon answered. Arranging the chairs before the meeting has been a waste of time. Everyone is on the carpet again, most prostrate before the Lord. More repentance. More Scriptures spoken under the anointing of the Spirit, the same sense of the Holy Presence of Jesus; more worship of Him in His holiness.

One by one others were breaking through to a new place of

holiness with God and they were being liberated to a new place of adoration and worship. The time pased so quickly: one hour, two, three, four hours. There is little sense of time before the throne of God.

Monday was a Bank Holiday, and we could spend some time with our children. At seven p.m. we were back in the library. David Brown had taken a small group to Yorkshire to lead a parish conference. The team had arrived home in the afternoon and immediately sensed that things were different; the people around had changed. Later he was to say that his reactions were a mixture of longing and fear. He longed to be in that place where God had led others in his household. Yet there was a genuine fear of meeting the Lord in this way, a fear of the cost, of what he would have to face personally. It appeared to him that in one weekend those whom he was leading as pastor of the community had overtaken him. It was not long before he and the others were on their faces before the holy presence of Jesus.

As on the previous two evenings there was open repentance, leading to a great sense of the Lord's peace and worship before His throne. But then the unexpected happened. The room was not only filled with the holiness of God, but with His glory!

It has been difficult enough to explain events so far; now no words can be found to describe what followed. People were no longer on their faces; everyone was standing, arms extended to heaven, exalting God with loud voices, shouting praises to Him. And He was there in majesty, in glory, in honour.

I felt as if I was in the crowd shouting "Hosanna to the King!" There was sense of inexpressible joy. It wouldn't matter if there was never to be another time like that during my earthly life. I had known glimpses of the Lord's glory before, even a foretaste of heaven, but nothing quite like those minutes. One thing I knew for certain. I would never be the same again.

> Day and night they never stop saying:
> Holy, holy, holy,
> is the Lord God Almighty,

who was, and is, and is to come.
Whenever the living creatures give glory, honour and
thanks to him who sits on the throne and who lives for
ever and ever, the twenty-four elders fall down before
him who sits on the throne, and worship him who lives
for ever and ever.
(Rev. 4:8–10).

14   The Warehouse Floor

IN FACT, none of us would be the same again, although we were quick to realise that what had happened was a threshold to new things, rather than an end in itself.

On the following day the mission team began a tour of the country for a series of ministers' meetings and rallies: Grimsby, Southport, Blackpool, South Wales, Bracknell. Already we noticed that things were different.

A Spirit of prayer had come upon us, such as we had not known before. We were used to praising the Lord on our journeys and spending some of the time in prayer. Now there was nothing we wanted to do except pray, a deep intercessory prayer pleading on behalf of the Church and those who were lost in each of the places to which we were going; prayer for the nation and the work of spiritual revival.

It had been our custom to pray for half an hour together as a team before an evening meeting. Now we wanted two hours, and we were quick to be on our faces before the holy presence of Jesus, inviting Him to deal with us in any way necessary, so that there would be nothing to hinder the flow of the Holy Spirit's activity in our ministries.

Open confession of sin came naturally and spontaneously. There was no point in trying to hide anything from God or one another. At the pre-mission rally in Pontyclun, South Wales, we were meeting in a small church building. The only convenient place to pray was in the church itself. As we came through the cross into the glorious presence of the risen Lord, people began to arrive for the service. The Spirit of worship took hold of them and they joined in. That meeting never had a beginning. Four hundred people packed into the building and were caught up in praise and adoration from the start. There was obviously going to be one problem in that area: finding a big enough building for the mission itself.

Once again we were beginners. "Lord, how do we lead people to seek you in your holiness?" Gradually we learned the answer to our question as the weeks of ministry passed.

Immediately after that brisk tour, the mission to Hemel Hempstead began. There was a keen sense of anticipation among the team. This mission was surely going to be different from any we had known previously. Was there going to be the mighty move of God so often associated with revival? Were we going to see hundreds flocking into the Kingdom of God each evening?

The meetings took place in the large public concert hall in Hemel Hempstead. Two memories stand out for me. The first is the hours of prayer we spent on the hard, cold floor of one of the dressing rooms; hours of praying with an intensity we had never known before.

The second memory flows from the first. It was the penultimate night of the mission. Many had received personal blessing during the previous evenings, but we sensed that a spiritual breakthrough was needed in this town. The victory had to be won in prayer. We needed to see God moving in a different way, although we could not be specific about what that meant.

As we drew into the holy presence of God we saw the situation about which we were praying through His eyes; we even felt as He did. Those with a ministry of intercession will readily identify with what I am saying. The Holy Spirit prays in you and through you with His understanding of the situation.

I had never experienced this with the intensity that I was aware of on this particular occasion. A great sense of the Lord's grief came upon me. He showed me that it was His Church, more than the lost, that grieved Him. I found myself pleading before the throne of God for the churches of that area, crying out for Him to have mercy on His people. I wanted to pray for all who didn't know the Lord, but the Spirit would not lift this burden of grief over the churches.

It was nearly time for the meeting to begin. How could I preach with this tremendous burden of prayer upon me? We made our way from the dressing room onto the stage. "Be prepared for anything," I said to Kevin. "I don't know what is going to happen, but I sense it's going to be different." After the opening hymn I came forward to one of the microphones and called the people to prayer.

I was told afterwards that I led in prayer for nearly an hour — not the usual way to conduct a mission service. When I opened my eyes and looked around the hall I was amazed. About fifty people had come forward to commit themselves to Jesus, acknowledging His total claim upon their lives. In addition, the aisles were littered with people on their knees and faces before God. In a concert hall there are no facilities for kneeling; yet many of those still remaining in their places were on their knees. There was that sense of the awesome, holy presence of Jesus.

This is what I had read about in books on revival. The real business of the evening had happened, not through any mighty preaching of the Word, but through prayer. "Glory be to you, Lord."

One of those present wrote: "We were conscious of God breaking us of our stubborn pride and rebellion, disobedience and selfishness, and bringing us to a new place of intercession for the lost and the reviving of God's church."

The mission in Luton was held in the football stadium, by kind permission of the Luton Town Football Club, who were most helpful to us in all our preparations.

It was nearly six years since I had left the town. Returning to lead the mission had naturally created a considerable amount of local interest, not least from the press. St. Hugh's was among the churches that had prayed and prepared with zeal, believing that the Spirit of the Lord would move mightily in those days.

One of the most significant aspects of that mission was the

morning prayer meeting when several ministers and local leaders joined the team in seeking the Lord in His holiness.

The venue of each mission was to have a considerable effect upon the kind of people who came. Those held in churches attracted mainly churchgoing people and unconverted friends whom they invited. Those held in public halls attracted a wider audience — people who would be used to attending such places for other functions. None of the other venues attracted a greater cross-section than the football ground at Luton. This was truly neutral ground. We heard of a number who came only because the mission was held there, and some of them met with the Lord.

The spring and early summer had been extremely wet. It was important that the weather remain dry in such an exposed place. This was a matter of prayer and the Lord answered. Every evening was dry. The last meeting was held on the Saturday afternoon and that, too, was fine. But as the meeting drew to a close the storm clouds were gathering. "Lord, please keep the rain away until we have finished." Five minutes after the close of the meeting the heavens opened and the rain poured down. Praise God the heavens had been opened spiritually all week.

The Football Club were pleased with the dry weather too, as their pitch was having a new drainage system installed. It enabled the work to go on unhindered. I told their representative, himself a Spirit-filled Christian, that the Lord would give back to the club as it had provided generously their facilities for the Lord's work. I suggested that they would gain promotion from the Second to the First Division of the Football League. At the moment of writing they are seven points clear at the top of the table with three games in hand over their nearest rivals! We are expecting all the other Second Division clubs to invite us to hold missions on their grounds! (See note at end of chapter.)

After Luton, we went the following week to Grimsby, for the Humberside mission. This was held in the "Ice House", recently converted into a meeting hall and Christian Centre. The dressing room here was far more comfortable than the one at

Hemel Hempstead; it had carpet on the floor. Spending so much time on our knees and prostrate before the Lord, we appreciated such luxury.

The Holy Spirit had moved with power during the pre-mission rally here, and many people received great blessing in the early evenings of the mission. Again we were conscious of the need for a spiritual breakthrough. Spiritually, the Grimsby area was noted as being one of the toughest in the country. The holiness of God had to be manifested in some way to bring people to a new place with Him. We were learning that the only way for this to happen was for us as the team to seek Him ourselves with all our hearts.

It was a great incentive to know that so much depended upon our willingness to seek the Lord. We were not seeking Him for ourselves but for His sake and that His finest purposes might be fulfilled among the people. This seeking had to be centred upon Him, not upon ourselves. We would praise and worship Him in English and in tongues. Within a few minutes we would be bowed low before His holy presence. We would be able to go no further until the Holy Spirit had convicted us of any sin or wrong motives and had dealt with any lack of unity between us, no matter how trivial the matter might seem.

We learned to repent quickly of these things, allowing the Lord to bring us to peace and liberty so that we could pray through to victory for the meeting. Often people cannot receive the victory in prayer because they bury their sin and the niggling things that divide them. Until those things are dealt with, there cannot be the true unity that the Lord desires to see among His children as they approach His throne in prayer.

Then followed a time of battling in the heavenly places in prayer. Paul reminds us: "For our struggle is not against flesh and blood, but against the rulers, against the authorities, against the powers of this dark world and against the spiritual forces of evil in the heavenly realms." (Eph. 6:12)

During this time we used the prayer gifts. It does not make sense to try and achieve victory in your own strengths, without using the resources God makes available to you. There would be much praying in tongues, as the Spirit understands how to pray better than we do, especially when the victory of Jesus is being proclaimed over "the spiritual forces of evil in the heavenly realms".

God would lead us to pray for specific areas relating to the meeting. There would be several passages of Scripture given by the Spirit, as well as prophetic words and visions. All this after inviting the Lord to give us His burden for the meeting and the area, and not to release us from prayer until we knew that we had reached the point where He wanted to take us.

Whatever happened in the service would be a direct reflection of the point to which we had prayed through. Sometimes we could only reach a place of peace, not victory. God would work among His people, but that would not be the same as praying through to a place of victory when the Lord would reveal His holiness and glory among His people. Every time we could get to that point in prayer, we knew that a revival meeting would follow.

Already, in Grimsby, we had spent many hours in prayer to break the spiritual oppression over that town. We had not reached that place of victory for which we longed, and which we knew to be the Lord's purpose. We must have that victory; nothing less would do. God had to come among His people in His holiness. We told Him that we were prepared to continue praying until we were assured of that victory; it seemed pointless to have just another night of blessing and miss God's best. It has been said that in spiritual things, the good is the enemy of the best.

The breakthrough came at seven-twenty p.m.; the meeting was due to start at seven-thirty. How did we know that we had the victory? All of us together at the same time came through to a sense of the glory of God in our midst. Instead of being on our faces before Him, we were now on our feet shouting His praises. There was that awesome sense of the holy presence of God, something that cannot be imagined or manufactured.

That holy presence was in the dressing-room and we knew that God would be present in that same way in the meeting. The members of the team made their way quietly to their places. There was only time for Kevin to lead two brief choruses, instead of the fifteen minutes of singing that was usual before the meeting formally began.

Yet in those few minutes of singing I was aware of that same awesome presence of Jesus. At the beginning of each meeting Charles Sibthorpe had to make his way from the piano to the lectern to give out notices and introduce the meeting. On this occasion, he seemed reluctant to do so. He looked across to me. I was so awestruck by the Lord's presence I couldn't speak. Nor could he when he arrived at the lectern. Finally he blurted out: "By the time this meeting ends, I believe it will be totally irrelevant that the bookstall is on this side and the tapes available over there." And he returned to the piano. That was no way to give out notices; but how right he was in what he said.

As the meeting concluded, people streamed to the front, weeping and kneeling before the Lord. They were meeting with Him in His holiness and power. "Will you come and teach my church how to pray?" one minister asked me. He realised where the secret lay.

Blackpool in the holiday season, the church in the middle of the town packed with hundreds of residents and visitors every night. On one evening there were at least 300 people kneeling all over the place praying that the fire of God's Spirit would come upon them, to purge and cleanse them from all that was unholy and to give them hearts that wanted to live in holy obedience to Him.

It is important in our Christian growth that we do not lose dimensions of life previously experienced and enjoyed, simply because God is opening up a new and different dimension. God does not want us to have love or faith, wisdom or courage, holiness or power. He wants His children to know His love and faith and wisdom and courage and holiness and power.

As people were led to seek the revelation of the Lord in His holiness, the works of power continued to happen. He is always willing to confirm His word with signs following. In fact the revelation of God's holiness led to an increase in the evidence of that power, in ways that would encourage others in their faith. Ernie was such an example.

He had limped into the meeting on the previous evening, crippled with arthritis and using a heavy stick. He had left the meeting running and "bouncing about like a rubber ball". As he gave his testimony, he jumped up and down on the platform to demonstrate his healing to the whole gathering. For years he had been in great pain with his affliction, but on the previous evening God had spoken to him about putting things right between himself and God, and in his attitude towards others. As he did that in prayer, so the Lord met Him in His healing power. Another fruit of seeking the holiness of God.

Things were different, too, back at The Hyde. On the day after the community's "revival weekend" there was the usual Tuesday evening open meeting. On that occasion I was told that some were on their knees and faces before God, crying to Him for His mercy. Somehow the holy presence of the Lord among members of the community helped to bring others to conviction of their unholiness. Others began to seek Him for a further breakthrough in their lives.

On the following Sunday, I was at home between missions. During the Communion service a young housewife who was visiting us broke down in tears. When I spoke to her afterwards she told me: "I felt so dirty among such clean people." She knew nothing about what had happened to us only a few days before and was herself a beautiful Spirit-filled believer. As a result of our conversation, she saw her need to come into a new place with God.

I was beginning to see why the books about revival spoke of people coming so readily to conviction because of the holiness of the Lord's presence among believers. This was further enhanced by a casual remark from another regular visitor to the community. "I always enjoy the drive here; but today it was different. The nearer I came to the house, the nearer I was coming to the holy presence of the Lord. When I arrived I seemed to be walking on holy ground." Nobody had said that before.

It was immediately apparent that we not only had to stay in the place to which God had brought us, we had to move on with Him. Only then would we be able to lead others into a new holiness of life. It would be so easy to slip back. The Lord was speaking to us very clearly about the need to "walk in the light".

This is the message we have heard from him and declare to you: God is light, in him there is no darkness at all. If we claim to have fellowship with him yet walk in the darkness, we lie and do not live by the trust. But if we walk in the light, as he is in the light, we have fellowship with one another, and the blood of Jesus, his Son, purifies us from every sin. (1 John 1:5–7)

To walk in the light meant that we had nothing to hide from one another. To be like Jesus, to be living in His holiness, affected not only our relationship with God, but with others too. In fact, holiness is something that could only be demonstrated in relationship with others.

Therefore, as God's chosen people, holy and dearly loved, clothe yourselves with compassion, kindness, humility, gentleness and patience. Bear with each other and forgive whatever grievances you may have against one another. Forgive as the Lord forgave you. And over all these virtues put on love, which binds them all together in perfect unity. (Col. 3:12–14)

That began on our knees. The mission team was discovering the vital significance of sharing open confession of sin, as the Spirit led us. This cannot be a legalistic device to try to win favour with God. It has to come spontaneously from the heart in response to the prompting of the Holy Spirit. To resist is to block the flow of the Spirit, not only in the time of prayer, but in your relationships and life generally.

Such openness can only happen with confidence if there is mutual love among the brethren, not criticism or judgment of one another. That would only happen if the people concerned had not truly met with the Lord in His holiness. Certainly nobody would dream of talking to others about what was confessed. Everybody concerned needs to be in that place of seeking the Lord, of being open with Him and others — not sitting in judgment upon their brethren.

Having begun to walk in the light, there is the constant temptation to retreat from that position, to retreat back into oneself, thinking that the Lord knows and the Lord forgives, and that is all that matters. Jesus would not agree with that. It is only those who love the shameful deeds of darkness who seek to hide. "Everyone who does evil hates the light, and will not come into the light for fear that his deeds will be exposed. But whoever lives by the truth comes into the light, so that it may be seen plainly that what he has done has been done through God." (John 3:20–21)

Since that initial encounter with the holiness of God, we have sought to live in the light with one another. The community has grown to such a size that this can only be done meaningfully in small fellowship groups or life-cells. In these there is not only a mutual sharing of sin, but a sharing of the new life of Jesus, building and encouraging each other in faith, and caring for one another at the level of practical need.

The whole community has become increasingly evangelistic, by its lifestyle as well as by its ministry. Several people have come to us in great need, some with devastated, shattered lives. The openness among others has enabled them to be open about their needs and the darkness in which they have lived in the past. This has led to so much healing that they stay on as members of the Fellowship.

Henry Lambert-Smith's healing was recorded earlier. He came to spend some weeks with the community and shared in several of the missions described. He writes:

My impressions of the Bethany Fellowship are of two kinds. The atmosphere of love and acceptance at once made me feel at home.

Bethany's Christianity is real and practical. Walking in the light, with open confession of sins, and forgiveness from God and the Community, keeps relationships harmonious and loving.

A week at The Hyde leaves an impression of deep-seated contentment, an awareness of God's presence. A sheltered atmosphere, you may say. "They can know nothing of the world and its problems."

Then Colin took me out with the Mission Team, and showed me the very powerful thrust into the outside world. The Good News is taken to those in need. The cross is central, and always the congregations are invited to give their hearts to Jesus, out of gratitude for His once-for-all sacrifice, and His continuing love.

Colin believes that the message of salvation is incomplete without accompanying signs. (Mark 16:20) So he lets it be known that God desires to show His love by healing. I have seen literally hundreds of healings, some purely physical, like the Blackpool man crippled with arthritis. There were healings of the emotions, depression, feelings of rejection, relationships, marriages. Such experiences are a powerful help to faith. God is great. He loves His children. He is able to help us in all circumstances. Nothing is too hard for our heavenly Father.

We greatly valued Henry's contribution of prayer and devotion to the Word of God. Whoever comes among us can be a source of blessing as well as someone who, we trust, will meet with the Lord and be blessed by Him.

In the summer I made a further visit to Switzerland and a return to La Porte Ouverte Conference at Chalon, France. I had the great joy of taking my elder daughter, Claire, who was then fifteen years old. Cathy, another member of the community who speaks French, also came with us.

In Geneva, we were with a team of young people from Youth With A Mission (Y.W.A.M.) who were preparing for a period of street evangelism in the city. The message about living in the light went straight to the hearts of those young people. How can we expect to bring the light of Jesus into the darkness of other people's lives, unless we are living in the light ourselves? And we shared with them the importance of praying through to victory. As we sought the Lord together He touched many lives. One young man had been hobbling around on crutches, his leg heavily strapped. He felt a great sense of failure and was about to pack his bag and go home defeated. How could he be a witness to Jesus, who he believed to be mighty in healing power, when he so obviously needed healing himself? The Lord had mercy on him and completely healed his leg to the joy of the whole group.

Not holiness or power; holiness and power. They go together in the life of Jesus. They need to be together in the ministry of His Body.

After that prolonged healing meeting during my last visit, what was going to happen this time at La Porte Ouverte? Once again I was asked to minister at the healing session, but this time I used the word of knowledge ministry. Hundreds were healed, and it didn't take nearly so long; neither was I so exhausted at the end.

Further Kingdom Faith Missions took place in the autumn. The climax at Manchester was the final meeting at the Free Trade Hall. About 150 indicated that they had given their lives to Jesus for the first time; many hundreds of others came to a new place with God. About 1500 stood to ask God to fill them with the Holy Spirit and well over a thousand indicated that they had received the healing power of Jesus. We had never known such a victory prayer time before that meeting, and that victory was manifested in the events that took place.

Behind the scenes, during the earlier part of the week, the team was again spending many hours battling away in prayer over the spiritual climate of that large city. We were discovering the cost of seeing God move in greater power, but we did not begrudge that at all. The Lord has called us to seek first His Kingdom and His righteousness; our lives are given to Him for His purpose.

The Lord had taught us an important lesson about seeking His Kingdom first. The members of the community had all enjoyed a time of holiday, much needed as the pressure of events around The Hyde was growing continually. As we came together again, there was not quite the same sense of holiness and liberty. Something was wrong. The Lord thought so too, because the financial supply for the ministry began to run dry. We now needed around £3,000 a week to maintain all the aspects of the ministry as well as capital sums to buy further properties to house the enlarging community. And still we did not feel it right to ask for money or make our needs known to men, but only to our heavenly Father.

He was obviously not pleased about something. We had a day of prayer and fasting to seek Him. He showed us that we were not walking in the light fully, with that same openness that we had experienced during the summer. While away from each other during the holiday period we had unwittingly shrunk back from that complete openness that we had known.

We were drawn to a fresh repentance, a renewed commitment to walk in the light. On the following morning gifts amounting to several thousands of pounds arrived in the post. I love the Lord's sense of timing!

We had never battled harder in prayer that we did at Pontyclun. The mission to Mid-Glamorgan was centred on this village because of its strategic position within easy reach of many large towns, but also because some local Christians felt that God was wanting the churches and chapels there to work together. I was assured by many people with a life-long knowledge of the area, that such a thing had *never* happened before. Now, amazingly, they were not only working together, but were doing so on an evangelistic campaign. And that is the most difficult area in which to get co-operation between churches.

However, there was not an ecclesiastical or public building of sufficient size for the mission for miles around. The local committee had made this a principal topic of prayer; and God, of course, answered. A factory closed down and was to be converted into a warehouse. For the duration of the mission it would be empty and we were welcome to use it. The owners hurriedly had new toilet facilities installed in time for the mission.

As the factory had produced lead pencils, local church people had worked hard to remove the bulk of the graphite dust — a filthy job. A platform festooned with flowers was erected and dozens of posters decorated the walls. Chairs were borrowed and there was the ideal meeting place — except that it was October and there was no heating.

But people came prepared. They were not going to allow the cold to keep them away from what God was going to do. In that immediate area there were very few people that had any experience of renewal in the Holy Spirit, and Kevin's anointing to lead people to a place of praise was needed. Ruth Fazal had flown from Canada for these missions and ministered beautifully with her violin and in song.

As with former missions, the first three evenings saw blessing, but we had not been able to pray through to a place of victory. On the Friday, we knew that we must meet with God in such a way that we would see the spiritual breakthrough so needed in the mission.

I was deep in prayer, pleading for the people of that area when suddenly I saw the Lord Jesus, not physically, nor in imagination but with the eye of the Spirit. There had been a few precious occasions when God had given me that privilege and all of them had been joyful, glorious experiences. But not this one. Jesus was walking away from me.

I cried out in great distress. The others could not know what I was experiencing, but they must have been aware of my great anguish. "Lord, you can't leave. You can't, Lord. You must not, Lord. It is all hopeless without you. You can't leave." I pleaded and pleaded with Him. If I could physically have reached out to restrain Him I would have done so. He was not walking away from me personally but from the situation. That did not prevent the intensity of my pleading, for when interceding we became indentified with the place and the people among whom we were ministering.

After a while the Lord stopped and He looked at me. His face was gaunt, the eyes sunken; His expression one of total grief.

"My people here do not want me," He said, and turned away again.

My pleading became more frantic and I produced all the Scriptural arguments I could think of. What about the lost? What about the righteous ones? What about those who were prepared to be obedient? "Lord, you cannot leave us."

After a while He turned towards me again. "I will tarry for these two days," He said, and then disappeared.

Although the room was cool, I felt bathed in perspiration and exhausted with the pleading. It was some time before I could speak and even then could not bring myself to tell the others what had happened. Ringing in my ears were those words I had heard, "I will tarry for these two days." They were words of hope, of promise. "Tarry" is not a word that I would ever use myself and I was struck by the Lord's use of it. How could I preach after an experience like that? During the first part of the meeting I sat on the platform, still in a daze. To share in the Lord's feelings about a situation so completely had proved devastating.

When it was time for me to speak, I shared what had happened in prayer and the Lord showed people that although many were well conversant with His Word, they did not want to face up to the implications of living it, of bring committed to Him and to one another.

What a contrast to the previous evening when the theme of the message had been: "Fear not". And yet how scriptural. At one time Jesus would be saying "Fear not" to His disciples; at another He would be referring to them as "a perverse and faithless generation".

On this occasion, the response of people was different from the previous evenings, when many had sat listening without appearing to respond in any way to the gospel of life and truth. Now, however, many did respond with genuine repentance. Frankly, I was amazed that still there were a number who appeared untouched by what was happening around them. Many went home and to their knees in prayer. I heard of people praying into the night and of at least one woman praying through the night. And when God gets his people praying things can really begin to happen.

As we met to prepare for the final service, we knew that we needed that essential victory in prayer. As I knelt on the floor of that cold warehouse I was trying desperately to concentrate on the job in hand. And yet for half an hour all I could hear was "You are to write another book, the sequel to *When the Spirit comes*."

I tried to push the thought away. This was not the time to be thinking of books. Was this the enemy trying to distract me? I confessed to the others that I was finding it difficult to concentrate on praying for the meeting. Would they please pray for me? So much depended on this prayer time; we needed a revival meeting tonight.

The others duly prayed, but the thoughts about the book persisted. If this was the Lord, His sense of timing seemed to have deserted Him!

"All right, Lord, I will do as you say." I had to agree to write this book at the first opportunity. Immediately I was at peace. Soon we were in a place of victory for the meeting.

Of course, the Lord's sense of timing had not deserted Him. He knew what He needed to do to persuade me to write this book. In times of prayer like that, my resistence to Him is at its lowest. For some reason, that I could not appreciate then, this book must be important to His purposes.

And the meeting? The local people afterwards were saying: "This is how our parents described the revival to us." That part of Wales had known a great movement of revival in the early years of this century. That evening it was like ministering in an entirely different place to an entirely different group of people. That is the fruit of repentance.

For me personally, much happened on the floor of that warehouse in Pontyclun.

(Note. Luton Town won the Second Division Championship, were eight points clear of their nearest rivals and were duly promoted to the First Division.)

15 Faith for the Future

GOD'S WANTS TO renew His Church, that as the Body of Christ it may be effective in continuing the ministry of Jesus in the world; a people committed to one another and to Him, dedicated to the cause of the gospel, prepared to give themselves whole-heartedly to the extension of the Kingdom of God on earth.

I am deeply conscious of areas of my life where there needs to be an increase of faith, a greater dependence upon God and a bolder proclamation of His Word and purposes. That faith, dependence and boldness will need to come from a holy life.

My heart is set on becoming more like Jesus through the grace and power of the Holy Spirit. This will involve suffering as well as joy, learning to take rejection, persecution and abuse as He did. "Blessed are you when people insult you, persecute you and falsely say all kinds of evil against you because of me. Rejoice and be glad because great is your reward in heaven, for in the same way they persecuted the prophets who were before you." (Matt. 5:11, 12)

To learn to react in such circumstances as He did is part of the holiness of life that God requires, for "love is patient, love is kind. It does not envy, it does not boast, it is not proud. It is not rude, it is not self-seeking, it is not easily angered, it keeps no record of wrongs. Love does not delight in evil but rejoices with the truth. It always protects, always trusts, always hopes, always perseveres. Love never fails." (1 Cor. 13:4–8)

To live a life that is holy is to live a life of love. Such a life cannot be the accomplishment of self-effort; it can only happen through the Holy Spirit being manifested in the weakness of our human nature. That involves not only the constant indwelling of the Holy Spirit, but also the continuing emptying of self.

When our lives are filled with the Spirit of God, we receive the same resources as Jesus Himself had available throughout His earthly ministry. We do not reflect that life as He did, or bear the fruit that He produced, or accomplish the things that He performed because the life of self often prevents that flow of God's Spirit in our lives.

My prayer is that God will break me of every way in which that life of self obstructs His purpose and prevents Jesus from being manifested more fully in my weak human nature. I want him to deal with every trace of pride and selfishness, with wrong attitudes towards others, to remove every trace of criticism and judgment. I want him to deal with the unbelief that persists so that I can have greater faith for the future.

This is not a lonely personal quest for holiness, for I want the Lord to deal in the same way with my wife and children, with my household and all in the Bethany Fellowship. Corporately we will then manifest more of Jesus and can become a more effective instrument in praying for revival in this and other lands.

I am under no illusions about the cost that lies ahead if we are to see God move in sovereign ways, not only to bring renewal within the churches, but to affect deeply the spiritual life of the nation, to reach the lost with the good news of Jesus Christ. There have to be those who are prepared to face such cost.

The last few years have been a wonderful revelation of the love and faithfulness of our God, of His tender compassion and mercy. They have been years of teaching, of training and correction, for the Father disciplines the children He loves. I have seen much to rejoice over and be thankful for, as the Spirit of God has moved freely at meeting after meeting, blessing countless numbers of people. And I am left only with a sense of my total nothingness before Him.

To me, the greatest privilege is to have entrance into that

most Holy Place before His throne, to bow before Him in
adoration and worship, lost in wonder, love and praise. And
the most important task ahead is to continue to seek Him for
Himself, to draw closer to Him, to be more attentive to His
voice and obedient to His commands.

He is the Lord who encourages His children and I want to
be a better encourager of others. I desire to express His love
more freely, His peace and joy more fully. And I want to be
faithful, obedient to His sovereign purpose for my life.

One verse of Scripture is a constant challenge to me: "I tell
you the truth, anyone who has faith in me will do what I have
been doing. He will do even greater things than these, because
I am going to the Father." (John 14:12) That is the faith I need
for the future. Jesus says that anyone with such faith will do
what He has been doing.

I cannot look back on the past with any sense of pride and
satisfaction; I can only look forward with an eager determination
that, where previously faith has been lacking, now I shall have
a greater trust in the Lord Jesus and the promises of His word:
"He will do what I have been doing. He will do even greater
things than these, because I am going to the Father."

And Jesus followed those words with further promises: "And
I will do whatever you ask in my name, so that the Son may
bring glory to the Father. You may ask me for anything in my
name, and I will do it." (vv. 13, 14)

Having known the truth of those promises in experience, I
want to abide in those words and be increasingly effective in
intercession and ministry to others, more attentive to His voice
and sensitive to His Spirit.

The flesh fights against all the aspirations of the Spirit. God
has dealt the death-blow to that flesh-life on the cross and we
can count ourselves "dead to sin but alive to God in Christ
Jesus." (Rom. 6:11) Paul continues:

Therefore do not let sin reign in your mortal body so that
you obey its evil desires. Do not offer the parts of your body
to sin, as instruments of wickedness, but rather offer your-

selves to God, as those who have been brought from death to life; and offer the parts of your body to him as instruments of righteousness. (Rom. 6:12, 13)

God wants to give us all faith for the future, to believe that He will move among us in the coming years with greater power. He wants to give us His faith and teach us to see things as He sees them. He wants to bring us to the end of compromise in our lives and ministries. He calls all who belong to Him to be part of His building work as He fulfils His promise to build His Church. He wants our confidence to be in Him as we fulfil His commission to proclaim the gospel of the Kingdom of God, to make disciples, to heal the sick and give freely to others as He has given to us. He calls us to share His concern for the lost, to participate in the cost of intercession to break the hold the powers of darkness have over many who reject the Saviour.

He calls His people to a life of personal holiness, to walk in the light with one another. Then others will more readily come under conviction of their sin and be drawn to repentance.

This is the message we have heard from him and declare to you: God is light; in him there is no darkness at all. If we claim to have fellowship with him yet walk in the darkness, we lie and do not live by the truth. But if we walk in the light, as he is in the light, we have fellowship with one another, and the blood of Jesus, his Son purifies us from every sin. (1 John 1:5–7)

The challenges to faith in the future will be great, but Jesus is the Author and Perfecter of our faith. May we all have the courage and boldness to follow Him faithfully and obediently, no matter what the cost; the faith to withstand the pressures of the world, the flesh and devil; the faith not to compromise the purposes of God within His Church or miss the opportunities He gives to extend His Kingdom.

All you have made will praise you, O Lord;
   Your saints will extol you.
They will tell of the glory of your kingdom
   and speak of your might,
So that all men may know of your mighty acts
   and the glorious splendour of your kingdom.
your kingdom is an everlasting kingdom,
   and your dominion endures through all generations.

                                    (Ps. 145: 10–13)

What a privilege it is to be part of that Kingdom and to be called to serve the King of Heaven, to step out to face the future with confidence and faith in Him. And the glorious hope that awaits us! When we see Him as He is, we shall be like Him! Hallelujah! Only the almighty God would ever embark upon such a purpose, to take people like us with our sin, weakness and failure and change us from one degree of glory to another until finally we are like Him. The realisation that this is His purpose gives me faith for the future.

Only Almighty God would take the foolish things of the world to shame the wise, and the weak to shame the strong. "He chose the lowly things of this world and the despised things — and the things that are not — to nullify the things that are, so that no one may boast before him." (1 Cor. 1:28, 29) He is the God of grace who has given us all things in Jesus, every spiritual blessing in the heavenly places, even though we deserve nothing.

May the Holy Spirit of God witness the truth of His words to your heart and give you faith for the future.

COLIN URQUHART

When the Spirit Comes

'Something different was needed; not just praying for sick people, but healing them!'

When the Reverend Colin Urquhart began his ministry as parish priest of St. Hugh's, near Luton, on a large housing estate, he knew from the experience of his predecessors that life would be tough. Within four years, however, his church has changed beyond recognition as the members found themselves witnessing miracles of healing, and establishing new relationships with one another. God gave them a remarkable vision of love, community and service.

COLIN URQUHART

My Father is the Gardener

'*In the life of the Church today, an important spiritual renewal is taking place. This is the work of God the Holy Spirit.*'

Colin Urquhart shows how individuals and a local church can experience renewal. Problems and fears give way to blessings and joy as ordinary people experience the presence of an extraordinary God.

The drama of renewal is now being experienced by Christians all over the world.

COLIN URQUHART

Anything You Ask

This book is strong meat. It will be talked about, argued about, and can revolutionise your life.

Jesus makes many astonishing promises of the response that God's children can expect to their prayers. But experience, for many Christians, seems to fall far short. Why?

Here is the teaching of Jesus on prayer and faith. Colin Urquhart shows, with examples from his personal ministry, how people can learn to pray with faith and *see God answering their prayers.*

COLIN URQUHART

In Christ Jesus

'*Wherever I travel I come across "defeated" Christians. Should they have to resign themselves to such defeat? Is it possible to know victory over temptation, weakness, futility and spiritual inadequacy?*' *asks Colin Urquhart.*

In Christ Jesus offers, not new forms of healing or new prayer techniques, but a clear, thrilling statement of what God has done for mankind through Jesus. This book contains the heart of Colin Urquhart's teaching: how we can know Christ's power for ourselves.